BUILDING THE
FAITH
A HISTORY OF THE CHURCH

JOSEPH CHARLES BEACH

BUILDING THE FAITH
A HISTORY OF THE CHURCH

JOSEPH CHARLES BEACH

JOSEPH CHARLES BEACH

Joseph Charles Beach

617 Sweet Gum Drive

Euless, TX. 76039

https://josephbeach.com

817-905-1956

Because of the dynamic nature of the Internet, any web addresses or links contained in this book may have changed since publication and may no longer be valid. Any people depicted in stock imagery provided by Getty Images are models, and such images are being used for illustrative purposes only. Certain stock imagery © Getty Images.

Scripture quotations taken from the (NASB®) New American Standard Bible®, Copyright © 1960, 1971, 1977, 1995, 2020 by The Lockman Foundation. Used by permission. All rights reserved.

https://www.lockman.org

Scripture quotations marked (NLT) are taken from the Holy Bible, New Living Translation, copyright ©1996, 2004, 2015 by Tyndale House Foundation. Used by permission of Tyndale House Publishers, a Division of Tyndale House Ministries, Carol Stream, Illinois 60188. All rights reserved. Scripture taken from the New King James Version® Copyright © 1982 by Thomas Nelson. Used by permission. All rights reserved.

Library of Joseph Charles Beach rev. date: 6/10/2024

Table of Contents

INTRODUCTION

As a Christian, is it necessary to know the history of the church? Is it important? Will it change your life?

Well, perhaps not, but...

Some may have a desire to know how the faith developed over time, how it grew, how it survived, and why it has been so dominant in our western world.

Most Christians are familiar with the early events of the church, of Jesus birth, life, crucifixion, burial, resurrection, and ascension. Then there is the book of Acts which tells the story of the Apostles spreading the good news to the Jews and then the Gentiles. But what happened latter?

We are now twenty centuries into the story of the church, a long time away from that first century. Many events have happened since but do we need know about these events? Church history may be one of the most overlooked areas of study for modern Christians today. One of the reasons could be the thought of "why does it matter?" or if it matters, "why are we not taught about these events in church?"

Others may not be interested in church history because of its association with tradition. Instead of wanting to know the old paths traveled over and over again by godly men and women of previous eras, Christians today want something "more spiritual" or more meaningful.

In today's society, many place little value in history and see nothing to be gained from this ancient and obsolete knowledge. After all, we live in such a different world today so how are these events relevant to me today?

Perhaps we should look at church history in a different light. Perhaps from learning a little more about church history, we could gain a better understanding in defending and developing our own faith.

Perhaps we as Christians should look back at the life and example of men in the Old Testament such as Abraham and David. In the New Testament, Christians can study the life and teachings of Jesus, Paul, James, John, and Peter. The history of the church is rich with the teaching of men and woman who have held to biblical truth and defended the faith against attacks from within and without.

If you have ever wondered how the Bible came into existence, how certain books were chosen, why some were not, and how church doctrine was established and carried forward, then perhaps you may discover you do want to know more.

Church history helps God's people understand the movements and sins that

Christians have made throughout history. Biblical truth may be stated in fresh ways; however, Christians must remain faithful to the old paths of biblical truth. Abandoning the old paths of biblical orthodoxy for doctrinal novelty leads to false teaching. The church should respond to false teaching by confronting errant doctrine with the Word of God. During such times, the church is afforded the opportunity to clarify and expound on biblical truth for the benefit and spiritual growth of the Body of Christ.

Church history helps God's people develop a context for a biblical-theological approach to the Christian life and ministry. God's people have a message to proclaim in the gospel. Christians need to learn from those who have gone before us in the faith. This helps us from falling into doctrinal errors which are not new, but rather old errors stated in fresh ways.

The orthodox Christian is motivated by a desire to state old truths in fresh ways with a view to faithfulness to the Word of God. False teachers throughout the history of the church think their teaching is the latest and greatest thing, but in reality, are repeating old errors already dealt with by the church? In short, false teaching promotes pride while orthodoxy honors God and brings Him glory. Church history is relevant because of the Word of God. Faithful men and women have sought to take what they have studied in the Word, apply it to their lives, and to instruct the people of God. The relevancy and importance of church history cannot be stated enough.

This writing is not intended to be a fully detailed and deep study of church history, but it will cover the main events every Christian should be familiar with. There are many books already written that will give you a more detailed look into the history of the church. However, if you just want to know the basics and a quick summary of church history, then perhaps this book is for you.

You will get a quick glimpse of the early church as recorded in Acts, featuring Pentecost, the spread of the good news to the Gentiles, the establishment of the early churches, the first council in Jerusalem, Paul's missionary journeys, the growing church, the establishment of doctrine and the councils making church decisions, the battle from within the church, the external forces outside of the church, and the development of the many denominations within the church.

This should be a good place to start and then you will know if you want to take it deeper.

Throughout scripture, we are taught how remembering scripture and older traditions gives us a better understanding of our own faithfulness. As early as Eden, Eve listens to the serpent, gets a false idea of who she is and who God is, and loses out on God's true revelation.

Throughout the Old Testament, God calls his people to recall and retell his gracious saving acts. Yet Israel repeatedly forgets, fails, and strays. The New Testament is also clear: Historical events are at the heart of the good news.

Our mission as Christians should be to remember history and call the nations to repent and believe in the Christ. Even the development of post-apostolic doctrine involved history. The early church fathers and councils had to determine, for example, what it meant to say with historical confidence that Jesus was both God and man.

The doctrine of divine providence reminds us that human history is a giant canvas on which we see God paint his sovereign plan. History leads us to a grand understanding of Christ. God's people have borne witness to the truths of his power and lordship, the centrality of his saving work in Christ, and the hope offered freely in the gospel.

Since Pentecost, God has been demonstrating this grand story of redemption in real places populated by real people, in the church. As visible outposts of the kingdom of Christ, churches are where this one great story continually confronts and collides with the stories of this world and the present evil age. Church history tells the stories of that confrontation, in all of its beauty and messiness.

The church is historically unique. God enters into a particular covenant with this new people, through the saving work of his Son, and makes promises to them as revealed in scripture. Church history is the story of how God has guarded, purified, chastised, and strengthened his undeserving people.

Understanding the historical circumstances surrounding doctrinal formulation should make us better theologians. Sometimes, church history reminds us of the failures and shortcomings of many of our forebears, even our heroes. History reminds us that the perseverance of the church has never been dependent on any human being. We're all too frail and imperfect. The church of Jesus Christ is established, furthered, and guarded by the King himself.

The most convincing histories will be those that portray faults as well as virtues. Not only does a biblical doctrine of corrupt practices give us an appropriate skepticism, it also provides needed humility to acknowledge we lack authoritative certainty about what happened in the past. Church history is the story of your true community and family. This belief runs contrary to how we often understand ourselves. Our brothers and sisters from the previous nineteen centuries, for example, compose our spiritual family. Though separated by time, we share one Lord, one faith, one baptism. The bond we share in Christ is more real and enduring than the connection we have with our families in the flesh.

Humility and empathy are required. Before we too easily judge motives, prejudices, or intentions, we must ask how we would fare in others' shoes.

Honesty compels us to speak plainly when previous generations of Christians have erred (for example, anti-Semitism, persecution of religious minorities, slavery, white supremacy, and so on). But it should also cause us to speak with charity and empathy, recognizing we are not much different from them.

We understand that our knowledge is never full and always clouded. Due to our limited abilities and fallenness, we will always need further steps toward the truth. This pursuit requires hard work, original research, and a humble spirit.

The church of Jesus Christ remains, as always, a people called to faithfulness in this age as we await Christ's return and the consummation of his rule in the age to come. Church history is part of that work of both remembering and anticipating—of living between the times. We tell the truth about the past, give thanks for God's grace, and repent of our sin and failure. But we do it all through the eyes of faith and the gospel of hope.

Growing in our knowledge of God's involvement in redemptive history helps Christians to understand patterns of how He has worked in and through His people. Outside regularly reading and studying of Scripture, there is no greater subject for Christians to study than the history of the church. Christians have a long and rich intellectual and spiritual heritage that has explained, and defended biblical truth for over two thousand years.

The Church - First Century

When the fulness of the time had come, God sent forth His Son, made of a woman, made under the law, to redeem them that were under the law, that we might receive the adoption of sonship (Galatians 4:5). In accordance with prophetic announcements, He was born in Bethlehem as the Son of David, and, after John the Baptist, and the last of the prophets of the Old Covenant, had prepared His way by the preaching of repentance and the baptism of repentance, Jesus' earthly ministry began in the thirtieth year of His human life with His fulfilment by life and teaching of the law and the prophets.

The beginning of the New Testament church could be traced to the most controversial figure in human history: Jesus of Nazareth. He is from the royal house of David, the King of Judah. He was born of the Virgin Mary during the reign of Emperor Augustus in the Roman Empire and Herod the great King of Jews about 4 B.C. His ministry commenced about 27 A.D. He had twelve apostles as his chosen associates in his ministry. The biblical narrations in Matthew, Mark, Luke and John tell of the details of his ministry, passion and ascension. These biblical records attest to his claim of Messiahship and redeemer of the whole world. Source: A History of the Early church, (05 BC-AD 451), John A. Apeabu (Ph.D.). Department of Christian Religious Studies, Federal College of Education, Zaria. Ii, © 2020 John A. Apeabu (Ph. D)

With twelve chosen disciples He travelled up and down through the land of the Jews, preaching the kingdom of God, helping and healing, and by miracles and signs confirming His divine mission and doctrine.

The Pharisees contradicted and persecuted Him, the Sadducees disregarded Him, and the people hesitated between applauses and insults.

After three years' activity, amid the hosannas of the multitude, He made His royal entry into the city of Jerusalem, home of His kingly ancestors. But the same crowd, disappointed in their political and carnal Messianic expectations, a few days later raised the cry: Crucify Him, crucify Him! Thus, He suffered according to the gracious good pleasure of the Father the death of the cross for the sins of the world.

The Prince of life, however, could not be held in death. He burst through the barriers of the grave, and rose again on the third day. For forty days He lingered here below, promised His disciples the gift of His Holy Spirit, and commissioned them to preach the gospel to all the nations of the world.

Then upon His ascension He assumed the divine form of which He had emptied Himself during His incarnation, and sits now at the right hand of power as the Head of His church and the Lord of all that is named in heaven and on earth, until visibly and in glory, according to the promise, He returns again at the restitution of all things.

Before Jesus, the called-out people, went into a covenant relationship with God at Mount Sinai and they functioned as God's people in the Old Testament just as the church functions as God's people in the New Testament. The church, therefore constitutes the Israel of God in the New Testament.

The Christian church was born in a world that was already old. Several empires including Egypt, Babylon, Assyrian, Persia, and Greece have already risen and fallen many centuries before. However, at the birth of Christianity, the Roman Empire governed the then civilized world. Thus, the church of the New Testament first appeared in history in Israel.

Jesus Christ, is the head of the church. The church comes into existence when its leader Jesus Christ is born. The incarnation of the Eternal word of God which dwelt among men to reveal the glory of God.

The church focuses on the life and ministry of Jesus, his teachings and his message of the coming of the Kingdom of God. Jesus selects his first disciple and the ministry of Jesus starts in earnest.

Jesus promised to build his church after the appointment of the twelve disciples. He teaches them for three and a half years before he is betrayed and handed over and executed. At first the disciples go into hiding as they are afraid for their lives. However, Jesus, just as he promised them, rises from the grave and defeats Satan and death in a mighty blow. Upon seeing their resurrected leader, the disciples learn even more from Jesus in the next forty days before Jesus ascends into Heaven. They all lose their fear and begin the building of his church just as Jesus had instructed them to.

Pentecost

Pentecost is the event that ignited the church!

Before Jesus ascended into Heaven, he told his followers to wait in Jerusalem. They were to wait for their companion and comforter. This occurred around the year 30 A.D. While they were waiting, they were celebrating the Feast of Pentecost (or Feast of Weeks), which was one of the three holy seasons at which God required His people to appear before Him in the place which He had chosen (Deuteronomy 16).

Acts 2:1-4: When the day of Pentecost came, they were all together in one place. Suddenly a sound like a "mighty rushing wind" (wind is a common symbol for the Holy Spirit) and "tongues as of fire" appear. The gathered disciples were "filled with the Holy Spirit, and began to speak in other tongues as the Spirit gave them utterance."

Scripture goes on to say:

Acts 2:41: Those who accepted his (Peter's) message were baptized, and about three thousand were added to their number that day.

The three thousand who were saved and filled with the Holy Spirit included men from Parthians, Medes, Elamites; residents of Mesopotamia, Judea and Cappadocia, Pontus and Asia, Phrygia and Pamphylia, Egypt and the parts of Libya near Cyrene; visitors from Rome, Cretans and Arabs (Acts 2:9-11).

In Christian tradition, this event represents fulfillment of the promise that Christ will baptize his followers with the Holy Spirit.

The description from the book of in Acts evokes the symbolism of Jesus' baptism in the Jordan River, and the start of His ministry, by explicitly connecting the earlier prophecy of John the Baptist to the baptism of the disciples with the Holy Spirit on the day of Pentecost. The timing of this event during the law giving festival of Pentecost symbolizes both continuity with the giving of the law, but also the central role of the Holy Spirit for the early church. The central role of Christ in Christian faith signified a fundamental theological separation from the traditional Jewish faith, which was grounded in the Torah and Mosaic Law.

Peter's sermon in Acts 2:14–36 stresses the resurrection and exaltation. In his sermon, Peter quotes Joel 2:28–32 and Psalm 16 to indicate that first Pentecost marks the start of the Messianic Age. About one hundred and twenty followers of Christ (Acts 1:15) were present, including the twelve disciples (Matthias was Judas' replacement) (Acts 1:13, 26), Jesus' mother Mary, other female disciples and his brothers James and Jude (Acts 1:14). While those on whom the Spirit had descended were speaking in many languages, the Apostle Peter stood up with the eleven and proclaimed to the crowd that this event was the fulfillment of the prophecy.

In Acts 2:17, it reads: "'And in the last days,' God says, 'I will pour out my spirit upon every sort of flesh, and your sons and your daughters will prophesy and your young men will see visions and your old men will dream dreams." He also mentions (Acts 2:15) that it was the third hour of the day (about 9:00 am). Acts 2:41 then reports: "Then they that gladly received his word were baptized: and the same day there were added unto them about three thousand souls."

Early Church Growth

From there the church began to grow. The first use of the term "church" is found in Matthew 16:18. The next reference to the church is in Matthew 18:17. The faithful believers of the Lord's time existed as individual followers of Christ but became a nucleus of the church at its formation on the day of Pentecost. Followers of Jesus in the church were first referred to as Christians in the town of Antioch (Acts 11:26).

The church, therefore, can be described as true believers in Christ, baptized into the body of Christ by the Holy Spirit. After this, the Apostles went forth "into all the world," as their Master had ordered them, to preach the Gospel to everyone. Later Paul would take the gospel to Asia Minor, Greece, and to Rome, while the other Apostles were busily doing the same work in other countries.

We must remember the constant coming and going which took place in those days throughout the world, how Jews went up to keep the Passover and other feasts at Jerusalem; and how the Roman empire stretched from Britain to as far as Persia and Ethiopia, and people from all parts of it were continually going to Rome and returning. Merchants travelled from country to country and soldiers were sent into all quarters of the empire. Through these travels, knowledge of the Gospel would be spread, and soon it would take root in the great cities of Jerusalem and Rome.

The last chapter of the Acts leaves Paul in Rome, waiting for his trial on account of the things which the Jews had laid to his charge. There is reason to think that Paul had also visited Spain, as he had spoken of doing in his letter to the Romans (chapter 15). He was at last imprisoned again at Rome, where Emperor Nero persecuted the Christians very cruelly from 64 A.D. until his death in 68 A.D. It is believed that both Peter and Paul were put to death there in the year 68 A.D.

The bishops of Rome afterwards set up claims to great power and honor, because they said that Peter was the first bishop of their church, and that they were his successors.

11

All the Apostles, except John, were martyred (or put to death for the sake of the Gospel). James the Less, who was bishop of Jerusalem, and the brother of Jesus, was killed by the Jews in an uproar, around the year 62 A.D. Soon after this, the Romans sent their armies into Judea, and, after a bloody war, they took the city of Jerusalem, and destroyed the Jewish Temple in 70 A.D.

It was during Nero's persecution that John was banished to the island of Patmos, where he saw the visions which are described in his "Revelation." After his return from Patmos, he went about to all these churches, that he might repair the hurt which they had suffered in their persecution.

The Gospel had now made its way among the great people of the earth, as well as among the poor, who were the first to listen to it. There is a story that the emperor was told that some persons of the family of David were living in the Holy Land, and that he sent for them, because he was afraid the Jews should set them up as princes, and should rebel against his government. They were two grandchildren of Jude, who was one of Jesus' kinsmen, and therefore belonged to the house of David and the old kings of Judah. But these two were plain countrymen, who lived quietly and contentedly on their little farm, and were not likely to lead a rebellion, or to claim earthly kingdoms. And when they were carried before the emperor, they showed him their hands, which were rough and horny from working in the fields; and in answer to his questions about the kingdom of Christ, they said that it was not of this world, but spiritual and heavenly, and that it would appear at the end of the world, when the Savior would come again to judge both the living and the dead. The emperor saw that there was nothing to fear from them, and he let them go. Source: Sketches of Church History, from AD 33 to the Reformation — J. C. Roberston.

The focus of early church history includes the description of the world into which the church was born and other environmental factors that influenced the spread of Christianity. The church at this time was considered to be a sect of Judaism.

As the early apostles were martyred and fewer eye witness to Jesus existed, the new church Fathers began the formation of the New Testament Canon and doctrines of the church. The infant church at this period was characterized by severe persecutions and martyrdom of Christians by the Roman empire. Also, during this time, other external conflicts as well as internal problems within the church started to appear. The internal challenges posed by heretical sects gave birth to writers in the church and those that stood to defend the faith, and doctrine (orthodoxy) of the church.

Three cultures, Hebrew, Latin, and Greek, more than any other, prepared the whole world for the birth of the church in the first century. Firstly, the Hebrews in their spreading the gospel had carried with them into every place the understanding of the one true God: Jehovah. Also rooted in their understanding was the expectation of the end time kingdom of the Messiah. This was the ultimate hope of Israel and the light of the gentiles.

On the other hand, the Greek culture providing a matchless language that became the common tongue of the whole then known world. This was initially, the medium of the spoken apostolic proclamation and later the medium of written apostolic instruction. The morally bankrupt Greek culture in its exploitation, philosophy, and science had served to prove that the way was clearly paved for the bold declaration of the gospel: "There is no other name whereby we must be saved" (Acts 4:12).

Furthermore, the socio-economic, cultural and political position of the then Roman empire also contributed immensely in preparing the cradle for the early church. For instance, the network of transportation, postal, and communication systems and by its cultural laws and military fortitude, Rome had consolidated and compacted together the mass of humanity so that it could be more easily reached with the gospel of Christ.

The decadent, and bankrupt world was indeed prepared to hear the anointed declaration of Christ's exalted Lordship from the lips of that small group of men that Jesus had personally discipled and sent into the whole world (Matthew 28:19,20).

Before the reign of Caesar Augustus (27 B.C.-14 A.D.), movement around the empire to take the Gospel to various parts of the Empire would have been an almost impossible task. But after Pompey had cleared the pirates in the Mediterranean and the Roman Army had ensured peaceful traffic on the roads of Asia, Africa and Europe, it now became possible for the early Christians to move from one place to the other preaching the gospel in the whole of the empire.

The church was born at a time when the Roman Empire had harnessed all the ancient empires. The defeat of those nations made them lose confidence in their gods who could not deliver them from the hands of the Romans. The people yearned for a 'superior god' or a more spiritual religion that would satisfy their quest for a 'messiah' which was not to be meant by the already existing religions. The vacuum created was readily filled by the advent of Christianity. More so, that the mystery religion and Emperor Worship that the Romans used and to substitute the gods of the land had helped to prepare the way for the Christian message. The infant church certainly enjoyed a favorable political environment created by the Romans.

Quite unlike most pagan religions of the Mediterranean world that were polytheistic in nature, Judaism uncompromisingly emphasized sound spiritual monotheism. The Jews in their dispersions had carried with them into every captivity their understanding of the true God Jehovah and the concept of monotheism that were central in the religion of Israel.

The Jews had offered to the world the hope of a coming Messiah which was rooted in their understanding of the expectation of end–time kingdom of the Messiah. It constituted the ultimate hope of all Israel and the light for the Gentiles. The hope of a Messiah for the Jews had been communicated throughout the entire Roman world. It was at this back drop that one can rightly appreciate the declaration of Andrew when he said: 'we have found the Messiah which is being interpreted, the Christ' (John 1:41).

By the end of the first hundred years after our Savior's birth something was known of the Christian faith throughout all the Roman empire, and even in countries beyond it. Source: A History of the Early Church, (05 BC-AD 451), John A. Apeabu (Ph.D.). Department of Christian Religious Studies, Federal College of Education, Zaria. Ii, © 2020 John A. Apeabu (Ph. D)

The Jerusalem Church

Jerusalem is where the church began. Jesus had told His disciples to preach the gospel everywhere, but to start at Jerusalem (Acts 1:8). God, in His grace, extended the offer of forgiveness to the very people who had been most responsible for Christ's death; He granted the very city where the Lord was crucified the honor of becoming the birthplace of the church.

On the Day of Pentecost, the Holy Spirit came to indwell the disciples gathered in Jerusalem, and in His power the church began (Acts 2). Source: What is the history and significance of the church at Jerusalem? | GotQuestions.org

Jerusalem was the first Head Quarters of Christianity even though there was much persecution of the Christians. This ironic Holy City was notorious for killing the prophets of God. No wonder Jesus in the following words lamented the evil of the city:

"Jerusalem, Jerusalem, you who kill the prophets and stone those sent to you, how often I have longed to gather your children together, as a hen gathers her chicks under her wings, and you were not willing. Look, your house is left to you desolate. (Matthew 23:37-38).

However, even during the persecution, the church was still very active here before the Jewish war with Rome.

Jesus had given priority to the proclamation of the gospel to the Jews is undoubtedly clear in the scriptures (Luke 24:47; Matthew 10:5-7; Acts 1: 8). The establishment and planting of the church followed this divinely prescribed order that Jesus gave. It is therefore not surprising that the gospel was first preached in Jerusalem among the Jews by Peter on the day of Pentecost. Thus, the earliest members of the church were Jewish Christians who evangelized the Jews in Judea and Samaria. The first expression of Christianity was a product of Judaism. The church in Jerusalem remained pre-eminent and predominantly Jewish community between 30-44 A.D.

Three days after Jesus was crucified, the news that He was risen from the dead as He had promised began to spread around the city of Jerusalem. Some of His closest disciples began to attest to the undeniable authenticity of Christ's post resurrection appearance. Invariably, the bodily resurrection of Christ gave birth to a resurrection of faith of the early Disciples of Christ. It is doubtful if there would have been any Christianity without a firm belief by the early Disciples of Christ in the bodily resurrection of Jesus from the dead. Suffice it to state here that, what seemed to be the firm roots of the Christian faith (in its infancy), was the unshakable conviction of Jesus' victory over death and that He did appear to many of His disciples. The belief in Christ's resurrection is the most outstanding explanation one can give to account for how the small band of demoralized believers eventually emerged as a transformed, dynamic movement for the church.

The bold proclamation that Jesus was risen attracted a lot of followers from all parts of the Roman Empire. Many came to believe that Jesus was alive and that His death on the cross was part of God's redemptive plan to atone and save mankind from the penalty of sin. The fact of bodily resurrection of Jesus Christ did not only serve to build and strengthen the faith of His disciples, but also gave meaning to His death. Not only that, the "Great Commission" that fostered the spread of gospel around Asia Minor, and indeed the whole of the Roman Empire (the then whole world), has been historically pitched at Christ's post resurrection charge to His disciples.

Several events were identified with the first Christian church at Jerusalem. These include:

1. The replacement of Judas by Matthias;

2. The communal life of the early church including:

    a. steadfast doctrine;

    b. steadfast fellowship;

    c. steadfast breaking of bread from house to house;

    d. steadfast prayer;

    e. baptism of new converts and

    f. steadfast and joyful praise worship;

3. the arrest and the persecution of the disciples by the Jewish authorities. The persecution that ensued at this time produced the earliest Christian martyrs (Stephen and James) of the church;

4. the appointment of the seven deacons;

5. the planting of the church in Samaria and the consequent conversion of the Ethiopian eunuch.

6. the Holy Spirit was given position of prominence in the early church, especially after the out-pouring of the Holy Spirit. Hence, they depended on the Holy Spirit for power and guidance;

7. the early church experienced what could be described as a geo-metric growth. Converts were from all works of life including a great company of priests. Between Acts chapter one to Acts chapter five the membership of baptized members had risen from one hundred and twenty to quite above eight thousand: with the addition of three thousand and another five thousand and later multitudes Acts 4: 4; 5:14).

8. the early church had some mixed multitudes who thought to corrupt the church through deceits: people like Ananias and Sapphira and later Simon the sorcerer;

9. the experience of divine discipline on hypocritical members: Ananias and Sapphira and

10. it clearly meant the content of the message of the apostolic church: Christ the predicted Old Testament Messiah who was crucified; died and buried but resurrected on the third day for our justification, redemption, reconciliation and salvation.

In Jerusalem the Disciples of Jesus and their converts participated in the temple worship. A communal sharing of earthly goods, care for the poor, especially widows and orphans characterized their fellowship. Miracles and wonders were performed by the apostles who preached Jesus crucified, dead and resurrected. Pentecost took place in Jerusalem. As the disciples continued to preach in Jerusalem publicly and privately, with signs and wonders following, the church grew tremendously in Jerusalem. Dissension also arose because of unequal or unorganized distribution of provisions to the needy in the Jerusalem church. Prompt action was taken to remedy this. This led to the appointment of Stephen (the first Martyr) who was appointed along with six other deacons.

Formal meetings for the purpose of regulating the doctrine and discipline of the church were reoccurring features of the history of the church. Those types of meetings are called Councils or Synods. The first church Council was held in Jerusalem about 49 A.D.

The First Apostolic Council at Jerusalem (49 A.D.)

Between the first and second missionary journey of Apostle Paul and his team there was a church council in 49 A.D. in Jerusalem. At this first Council, Jewish customs, laws and religion were discussed from the agenda. In attendance were the apostles and elders in the Jerusalem church; Apostle Paul, Barnabas (Judas), Silas, and some brethren from the Antioch church.

The influx of the many Gentile converts gave rise to the question of the condition of accepting non-Jewish people into the Christian church that was previously a solely Jewish congregation. The ensued controversy on whether or not the Gentile converts should be circumcised necessitated the first apostolic council at Jerusalem in AD 49.

At that council, it was resolved that the Jewish requirement: such as circumcision should not be made a legalistic demand or pre-requisite for accepting the heathen Christian converts into fellowship. The Council however, warned that, the participation in pagan sacrifices and eating of meat sacrificed to idols as well as sexual immorality associated with idolatrous practices were unacceptable to the Christian faith.

Following the precedence of the conversion at the house of Cornelius, the unanimous decision of the council after much debates was that the Gentile converts into Christianity through faith in Christ should:

1. not be subjected to the circumcision rites of the Jews as a necessary pre-requisite for salvation.

2. abstain from meats sacrificed to idols and things strangled; and

3. also abstain from fornication

The decision of the council was communicated to the churches of the Gentiles through Apostle Paul and Silas. It is pertinent to note that these eventual unanimous decisions of the church were guided by the Holy Ghost. In other words, through the leadership of the Holy Ghost, certain restrictions were prescribed for the gentile Christians that would enable the Jewish Christians to live harmoniously with them. The Gentiles were therefore expected to abstain from activities and practices that were offensive to the Jews however, they were not constrained to adhere to Jewish rudiments of the law. The Churches were charged in addition to their faith in Christ Jesus to be willing to refrain from activities that do not promote chastity.

Consequent upon the first missionary outreach to the gentile nations, the infant church grew tremendously and began to accommodate the Gentiles into the household of God's people. It became clear that the church of God (i.e. God's people) was no longer a nationalistic entity but a universal assembly that embraces both the Gentiles and the Jews.

Many Jewish leaders were religious but they did not know God (Romans 9:1-3; 10:1-24). When Jesus came to explain the way to the Father, they (the Jews) rejected him. They rejected God's Precious Cornerstone. Consequently, once again they would be banished from their land.

Jesus warned when you see Jerusalem under siege you will know that its desolation is near. There would be great distress in the land and wrath against God's people. They would fall by the sword and will be taken prisoners to all nations. Jerusalem would be trampled by the gentiles until the times of gentile are fulfilled (Luke .21:20, 23, 24).

Jesus warned against playing a waiting game to see how things would develop. Jesus said to his disciples get out fast and do not hang about, pack up quickly. There was a brief window of opportunity for Christians to flee Jerusalem. Believers were to flee from the approaching Roman army as soon as they saw the sign of Mark 13:14.

God had spoken, had the people listened they would not have been caught unawares by the desolation that occurred in 70 A.D. but they refused to hearken to that grave warning.

The Roman army did not practice a swift "blitzkrieg" kind of warfare. Their movement tended to be cautious, methodical, and relentless.

When Titus besieged Jerusalem, over one million Jews died in the next five months. On August 6, 70 A.D. Roman forces invaded the temple and just as Jesus prophesied, not one stone was left upon another. Jerusalem was burned and little remained in the city.

After the death of James and within the climate of these upheavals, the church of Jerusalem elected as her Bishop Symeon of Klopa. The headquarters for the Jerusalem church was located far from the Holy City because if its destruction. Because the Christians took heart the message of Jesus to flee, very few Christians remained in the city. Most of the Christians fled to Pella of Decapolis which was built on the eastern bank of the river Jordan. This city bore the name of the ancient capital of Macedonia and was populated by Greeks, close to whom the persecuted Christians sought and received refuge and protection.

The Christian church continued to be in exile and far from the deserted Capital, while it was persecuted as much by the Romans as by the intransigent Jews who were causing internal dissentions in the church. This was happening because those Christians who came from them (Jews), insisted in preserving the Mosaic Law.

Although some of the Jews fled to Masada, the Jewish state went into extinction, not to return again until 1948.

After the departure of the Roman armies, the Christians returned to the ruins of Jerusalem. They settled in the small quarter on the hill of Sion, which during the siege had escaped the general destruction and in which there was a small church, the church of God. The church became the religious center of the Christians who immediately after their return from the Hellenistic Pella, re-organized the Christian community in Jerusalem. Source: John A. Apeabu (Ph.D.). Department of Christian Religious Studies, Federal College of Education, Zaria. Ii, © 2020 John A. Apeabu (Ph. D).

The New Churches

Antioch

Antioch of Syria became the second center of apostolic influence alongside the Jerusalem church. Antioch was one of the earliest centers for Christian activities. Biblical history given by Luke the writer of the book of Acts would credit the city with the first place the disciples of Jesus were called Christians (Acts 11:26). The apostles' missionary enterprise to the gentile nations was first initiated at Antioch. Bible history also holds that the Apostle Paul, Barnabas and John Mark began their missionary callings in this city. A little wonder that they always resorted to it as a base. This is obvious from the scriptural evidences of the instances of Paul's return to Antioch after his first and second missionary journeys (Acts 14:26-28). Similarly, from Antioch, Paul's third missionary journey was commissioned.

Antioch is closely connected with the history of the planting and establishment of Christianity in the gentile world. Peter was the first Bishop of Antioch, successively followed by Erodius and Ignatius. Antioch could be described as the location for new focus of the expanding kingdom of the Messiah. It became a pivotal point of Christianity after the martyrdom of Stephen at Jerusalem.

The disciples who found refuge in Antioch spoke the Good News to the gentile Greeks in Antioch. There was massive conversion of the gentiles. When the reports of the massive conversion in Antioch got back to Jerusalem, the church sent Barnabas to Greece. Barnabas' arrival sparked even more conversion. Consequently, the assistance of Paul was requested. For about a year, Paul and Barnabas did evangelism for the Lord in Antioch in the year 42 A.D. The church in Antioch grew rapidly with much impact on the whole city.

It is quite instructive to note that Antioch became so significant, that it served as a location for effective mobilization of believers to raise funds for indigent Christians in Jerusalem. Missionaries were also mobilized to thrust out to the gentile world at Antioch. This dramatic new phase in the life of Christ's church was not again traceable to Jerusalem but Antioch. The reasons for much effectiveness and enthusiasms in the church may not be unconnected with the gifted prophets, evangelists, pastors and teachers that the church was blessed with. Thus, Antioch like many other early Christian communities like Ephesus, Corinth, Philippi, Rome and Alexandria served as satellite centers for spreading Christianity in the early days of the church.

Antioch (Pisidia - Acts 13:13-52) Pisidian Antioch is located at the South Eastern bank of the Anthios River in Central Asia Minor. It is at the North East of modern Lake Egirdir. Though the founder of the city is not certain, historical traces point to Seleucus or the Seleucids. The church in Antioch (Pisidian Antioch) would have been planted in 47 A.D. or there about during the first missionary journey of Apostle Paul and Barnabas. Except for Pamphilids and Perga, Pisidia Antioch was the first Asian city Paul and his company reached out to during their journey after a successful outreach to Cyprus.

Ephesus

From Antioch, Paul's third missionary journey was commissioned. The fruit was the establishment of third dynamic center of influence i.e. the church at Ephesus. Ephesus was central to the spread of Christianity during the first century. Paul, John, and possibly even Jesus' mother, Mary, visited or lived here. Paul is known to have "rebuked the cults of Artemis, winning many Christian converts in the process."

This city was so important to the new movement that Scripture mentions Ephesus several times. Archaeological remains provide a glimpse into what life was like for the people who lived here 2,000 years ago.

For instance, the Book of Acts recounts how the Christians faced hostility from the Artemis worshipers, who not only feared a loss of income from the making and selling of idols but also believed in and feared Artemis. A riot broke out against the Christians, but the Ephesian authorities ordered the aggressors to raise their issues through the proper legal channels.

The gospel took root in a big city filled with influences from around the Roman Empire, where new Christians would be tempted by urban excesses and frightened by persecution. The faith of the Ephesians in spite of these challenges encouraged Paul, who "entered the synagogue and for three months spoke boldly, reasoning and persuading them about the kingdom of God" (Acts 19:8).

Although he sometimes faced violent resistance, "God was doing extraordinary miracles by the hands of Paul so that even handkerchiefs or aprons that had touched his skin were carried away to the sick, and their diseases left them, and the evil spirits came out of them (Acts 19:11-12).

Paul recognized the positive things going on at Ephesus: their toil and patient endurance, and how you cannot bear with those who are evil, as the writer of Revelation put it (Revelation 2:2); yet later, they abandoned "the love you had at first" (Revelation 2:4). His letter was probably an important reminder to a church that was losing its first zeal for Christ.

Christ's message overturned belief in pagan forms of worship, and the Spirit also brought many Jews to faith. One can see how diverse this city was, with people living or passing through from all over the Empire.

Ephesus was well placed to demonstrate what unity in Christ and obedience to his teachings would look like. If they had built each other up and lived what they preached, this would have impacted the densely populated world that was watching them. Source: https://www.christianity.com/wiki/bible/what-is-the-significance-of-the-church-of-ephesus-in-the-bible.html

Alexandria

Another city known for its significant contributions in the development of Christian theology of the infant church was Alexandria. The city was named after Alexander the Great, who authorized the foundation in 331 B.C., though he was never to see the city. The city of Alexandria had a cosmopolitan population that included Egyptians, Greeks and Jews. The official language however, was Hellenistic Greek.

History has it that, the Christian population of Alexandria during the first century AD stood at about 180,000 which was well over one third of the total population of the city. The origin of Christianity in Alexandria cannot be directly traced in the New Testament scriptures, as there is no direct reference or mention of the city in the New Testament. However, New Testament records hold that people from Egypt benefited from Peter's speech at Pentecost (Acts 2:10).

Church history clearly credited the planting of Christianity and the first church in the city to Mark around 42 A.D. Mark was succeeded by Anianus as the bishop of Alexandria in the eighth year of Nero (62-63 A.D.) due to Marks death as a martyr in Alexandra but Coptic tradition says that Mark was martyred in 68 A.D. Source: https://en.wikipedia.org/wiki/Church_of_Alexandria

Athens

Athens was a city famous for its philosophical ideas and highly idolatrous interest. It was named after a Greek goddess: Athene. This city was densely saturated with statues and altars of Greek and Roman deities as well as the statues of the deified Emperor Claudius and Augustus. Paul particularly took note of one of the altars of pagan worship and superscription that was dedicated to the unknown god (Acts 17:20). Paul perceiving their ignorance and took advantage of their superstitions and preached to them. While preaching, Paul was arrested being accused of introducing a strange god. He was taken to Areopagus (Acts 17:19) The Areopagus council was responsible for the introduction of foreign divinities in the city hence Paul probably was arraigned before this court. Evidence from the scripture shows that Paul had a breakthrough in this city with many converts.

Colossae

Colossae was a small town during the first century. It was situated near Phrygia. It is supposed that Paul passed through Colossae on his way to Ephesus during his third missionary journey (Acts 18:23; 19:1). It is not too certain who planted the church of Colossae. Some scholars favor Epaphras and others Paul. Colossae is said to be the home town of Philemon. From the content of Paul's letter to the Colossians, it is obvious that the church had faced doctrinal threat from a particular heretical sect, most likely the Gnostics or Hellenistic Judaism.

Corinth

Corinth, the largest and most important commercial city in the Roman Empire was not far from Athens. In short, it was about eighty kilometers from Athens. The city was named after a popular current grape grown around the city. Corinth was an important large commercial city. Paul must have visited this city during his second missionary journey. Corinth was commercially linked with international network of roads from Asia and Europe. The moral decadence associated with the Corinthian church may not be unconnected with the influx of vices and crimes that usually characterize urban centers.

The history of the church in Corinth dates back to 49 A.D. during Paul's second missionary journey. Corinth had a history of being, an exceptionally immoral city and it was filled with immorality in Paul's days. This is evident in Paul's statement "it is reported commonly that there is fornication among you and such fornication as is not so much named among gentiles, that one should have his father's wife" (1 Corinthians 5:1).

During the second missionary journey, Apostle Paul is said to have spent not less than one and half fruitful years in Corinth. It was at this time that Paul came in contact with Erastus an influential city treasurer (Romans 16:23; 2 Timothy 4:20; Acts 19:22), Crispus and all his household (Acts 18:8) and Titus Justus who was probably called by Roman name Gaius. It was at this point he had contact with Aquila and Priscilla (Acts 18:2). Paul's tremendous success and breakthrough in Corinth not minding his previous opposition, is quite instructive and challenging. Paul refused to be discouraged by the previous rejection of ministry and presence at Athens, and he did not see the need to flee the city as he did at Iconium (Acts 14). Neither was he driven out by irate synagogue members and civic leaders as he had been in some cities of Galatia and Macedonia (Acts 13:80; 14:19; 16:39). Nor did his new converts send him away for his own safety as they had previously done in Thessalonica and Berea (Acts 17: 10, 13, and 14).

Paul's persistency and triumph may not be unconnected with the fact that he had received a divine commission and encouragement which became impetus and the drive for success at Corinth. "The Lord spoke to Paul in the night by a vision, be not afraid, but speak and hold not thy peace: for I am with thee and no man shall set on thee to hurt thee: for I have much people in this city" (Acts 18:9- 10).

It is believed that it was only after a period of eighteen months in Corinth that Paul was arrested by proconsul Galileo. Even at that, no harm was done to him in Corinth in spite of all their plots. This was in accordance with the divine promise of God to him.

The area of Decapolis, word 'Deca' (ten) 'polis' (city). Hence, Decapolis literally refers to a region of ten cities. Administratively, Decapolis: including Damascus, Philadelphia, Raphara, Scythopolis, Gadara, Hypos, Dion, Pella, Garasa and Canatha were territories belonging to Syria. The region of Decapolis was far from being a federation though they shared common Hellenistic culture which distinguish them from the surrounding cities and countryside.

Philippi

Philippi is located toward Eastern Macedonia. It is said to have been founded by immigrants from Thrace. Philippi was popular for the abundant gold mines and springs of water. The city is said to have been named after Philip II of Macedon (the father of Alexander the Great). The official language of Philippi was Latin while the market language and that of the surrounding community was Greek. The city was linked with Neapolis ports (Acts 16:11).

The church at Philippi was born in about 49-50 A.D. following Paul's visit to Troas (Acts 16:8-10). Although Paul had humiliating treatment in Philippi (Acts 16:19-20; 1 Thessalonians 2:2), he nevertheless, had a successful ministry at Philippi that gave birth to the church in the city. Converted through Paul's ministry at Philippi were people like Lydia (whose house was used for church meetings and fellowship, the Philippian Jailor and his family (Acts 16:14-15, 27-34), Epaphroditus (Philippians 2:25- 30), Euodia and Syntyche (Philippians 4:1-3), and Clement who served in the ministry of Paul and Silas.

There are evidences in the scripture to suggest that the liberality of the Philippian brethren served to support the ministry of the Apostle immensely (Philippians 4:15-18). The church in Philippi, was very dear to Paul. So much so that he had to visit the church at least once and again after planting the church (1 Corinthians 16:5,6; 2 Corinthians 2:13; 7:5; Acts 20:1- 6). This was the church whose leadership constituted the audience of Paul's 'Epistles to the Philippians' which among all other things addressed the conflict among some workers in the church.

Church history has it that in the second century, particularly during the fierce persecution of the early church one of the church fathers that suffered martyrdom in Rome, passed through Philippi on his way. The Christians that were scattered by the persecution that ensued from the opposition of the Jews to Christian teachings in Jerusalem took the gospel to Samaria. This was pioneered by Philip. The Christian community in Samaria was not purely Jewish. The church in Samaria had some identical features with the church in Jerusalem:

1. Converts were immediately baptized in water.

2. Members were filled with Holy Spirit.

3. There were also mixed multitude of people like Simon the sorcerer

Samaria

Samaria, located in the center of a broad valley stretching towards the Mediterranean and near mountains Gerizim and Ebal. Samaria, during the Omri dynasty served as the third capital of the Northern kingdom (1 Kings 16:24), after Shechem under Jeroboam and Tirzah under Bashan. Archaeological discoveries have revealed significant traces of Israelites occupation of Samaria to the beginning of the reign of Omri up to the period of the Assyrian captivity when the city fell to Sennacherib of Assyrian in the invasion in 722 B.C. under Shalmaneser.

Biblical history has it that Rehoboam was installed as a king to succeed his father, Solomon, in Shechem very close to Samaria. North of Palestine. However, Jeroboam's revolt led the whole of the Northern kingdom into apostasy that induced almost all his successors to follow his examples of idolatry, false religion, corrupt and immoral practices. This became conspicuous during the Ommiad dynasty that ruled for not less than fifty years. Ahab in particular is said to have embodied the policies that merged the depraved practices of Tyrian Baal-worship with the pure worship of Holy God of Israel. Eventually, Samaria that was notorious for Jezebel's (King Ahab's wife's) promotion of Baal worship was burnt down with all the principal officers killed or exiled into captivity.

Biblical records show that Samaria was colonized by Assyrians who resettled a mixture of foreigners from different places including Mesopotamia and Antioch Samaria. Biblical records also indicated that the colonialist adopted false religion as they sought to practice their idolatrous faith alongside with Israel's Judaism. 'So, these nations feared the Lord and served their graven images both their children as did their fathers so do, they unto this day' (2 Kings 17:41). Biblical and historical records attest to the persistent hostility between the Israelites and the Samaritan up to the time of Jesus. For instances: They refused Jesus' passage through Samaria on His way to Jerusalem. And the disciples sought to invoke fire to consume the inhabitant of Samaria (Luke 9:51-56). The Samaritan woman's attitude to Jesus also helps to illustrate the existing hostility between the Jews and Samaritans.

When a Samaritan woman came to draw water, Jesus said to her, "Will you give me a drink?" (His disciples had gone into the town to buy food.) (John. 4: 7-8)

There are indications that Jesus did not align with these prejudicial attitudes towards the Samaritans. Contrary to the Jewish custom, He would even dare to initiate a conversation with a woman from Samaria and even went as far as unimaginable taboo of a male Jew throwing a question unto a Samaritan woman. Jesus, distancing Himself from the holier than thou attitude of the Jews, was able to lead many men of the city of Samaria to salvation. The healing of the leper also testified to Jesus positive attitude towards the Samaritans. He also commended the action of the Good Samaritan with a parable. Jesus visited Samaria on a number of occasions to preach the gospel in Samaria despite the accredited cultural hostilities.

Samaria has a significant role to play in the purpose of illustrating the acceptance of God's redemptive plan for mankind. It is therefore not surprising that Jesus' post resurrection commission to the disciples would specifically include the mission to the Samaria.

But you will receive power when the Holy Spirit comes on you; and you will be my witnesses in Jerusalem, and in all Judea and Samaria, and to the ends of the earth." (Acts 1:8).

This suggests that the gospel work must be of a necessity to cut across cultural differences and prejudices among homogeneous people and even heterogeneous. If we must succeed in the twenty-first century's endeavor of preaching and reaching out to all creatures in all nations to make disciples for Christ, we have to carefully tailor our ministries today in the light of Christ's cross-cultural ministry among the Samaritans.

Jericho

Jericho was one of the surviving ancient cities of the Bible land. The history of this world's oldest city dates back to 8,000 B.C. The city of Jericho was a strategic and inevitable entrance into the Promised Land for the wayfaring Israelites in their wilderness journey to the Promised Land. Even during Jesus earthly ministry, Jericho was one of the important cities he stopped over on his way to Jerusalem. Source: A History of the Early Church, (05 BC-AD 451), John A. Apeabu (Ph.D.). Department of Christian Religious Studies, Federal College of Education, Zaria. Ii, © 2020 John A. Apeabu (Ph. D)

Set apart to the work by the church by prayer and laying on of hands, Paul and Barnabas started from Antioch on their first missionary journey to Asia Minor in 48-50 A.D. Notwithstanding much opposition and actual persecution on the part of the enraged Jews, Paul founded mixed churches, composed principally of Gentile Christians, comprising congregations at Antioch in Pisidia, Iconium, Lystra, and Derbe. When Paul undertook his second missionary journey, 52-55 A.D., Barnabas separated himself from him because of his refusal to accept the company of his nephew John Mark, who had deserted them during their first journey, and along with Mark embarked upon an independent mission, beginning with his native country Cyprus; of the success of this mission nothing is known.

Paul's Missionary Journeys

The conversion of Saul (the Apostle Paul) marked and signaled the spread of the Christian Gospel message beyond the Jewish communities to the Gentile world. Thus, Paul pioneered the activities of the early church that took the gospel to the then known whole world, including Asia and Europe.

Paul was born and raised up in Tarsus (Act 21:39). His genealogy has been traced to the tribe of Benjamin (Romans 11:1) and has been described as a Hebrew of the Hebrew. Paul (Saul) was a student of Gamaliel (Act 22:3), belonging to the sect of Pharisee as a son of a Pharisee. He was quite zealous and enthusiastic about the Law of Moses. Hence, he persecuted the church that had no regard nor observed the Law. To this end he took part in the stoning of Stephen to death, made havoc of the church, imprisoned Christians, had some tortured and beaten to death. Paul who had never thought of conversion to the Christian faith, blasphemed, persecuted and voted against every course of the church until he was miraculously called by God. He was said to have been in the company of those that murdered Stephen. In short, he consulted and kept the raiment of those that killed Stephen.

His dramatic conversion meant much for the Early church. Paul was on his way to Damascus, in one of his persecution trips (Act 9). Damascus is the current capital of Syria. Saul (Apostle Paul) was on his way to hunt for those who followed the way of Jesus (Acts 9:2). As Paul drew near the city of Damascus, a light from heaven flashed on and around him that he could not resist. He fell-down blinded but heard a voice that called on him, saying Saul, Saul, why are you persecuting me'. Saul replied "who are you, Lord." Jesus answered: 'I am Jesus, whom you are persecuting" (Acts 9:5). Saul's persecution of the followers of Jesus tantamount to the persecution of Jesus. Paul was directed to go and meet one named Ananias who further instructed him and told him that he was a chosen vessel to make known the name of the Lord among the Gentiles (Acts 9:6-13). Paul heard and accepted Christ as Lord and Savior and regained his sight. He started to preach Christ at the Synagogues.

The book of Acts gives among all other things, a historical account of the missionary outreaches and journeys of Paul that are epitome of the early church's evangelization and the unprecedented planting of churches among the Gentile nations.

Paul's First Missionary Journey 46-48 A.D. - Act 13:1-14; 28

Paul's First missionary journey covered a period of two years that is about 46-48 A.D., and a distance of about 1,400 miles (2400 kilometers). The team initially consisted of Barnabas and Paul. The missionary journey took off from Antioch in Syria. Their first place of contact was Seleucia and from there they sailed to Cyprus (the hometown of Barnabas). At Cyprus, the team preached in the synagogue at Salamis. It was at this juncture that they had John Mark added to the team. It would seem as if the team had succeeded in planting a church in Salamis. Their next point of contact was Paphos. At Paphos, they had an encounter with a Jewish false prophet (a sorcerer) by name Elymas. Elymas was one of the government officials (probably one of the special advisers) of the Deputy of the nation by name Sargius Paulus. Elymas who had attempted to hinder Paul's mission through diabolical power was immediately plagued with blindness through the power of the Holy Spirit using Paul. This recorded miracle of blinding Elymas helped to win the Deputy of Paphos (who was greatly amazed) to Christ. From Paphos they came to Perga in Pamphylia where John Mark took a leave of the team and departed to Jerusalem. The team (that is Barnabas and Paul) proceeded to Antioch in Pisidia. At Antioch, there were Jews in this Gentile community. Hence, there was a Synagogue where they (Paul and Barnabas) had a Sabbath service. Paul was given the opportunity to exhort the worshippers in the congregation. The sermon of Paul at the synagogue had provoked some of the Jews to oppose and resist the gospel while the Gentiles (that is, the religious proselytes) believed the gospel. Eventually, there ensued a division between the Jews and the gentile proselytes in the city. Some of the Jews were however receptive to the gospel and accepted the Lord Jesus Christ as their Lord and personal Savior. Though, the leaders of the Jews were opposed to Paul's message. The team somehow concentrated on the Gentiles as they preached the gospel all around in that region. The Jews successfully stirred up opposition against the team and they were consequently expelled from their domain and they departed for Iconium.

At Iconium they had both the Jews and Greeks in their audience also. Many had believed the gospel seeing the miracle, signs and wonders through the missionary team. They spent a long period with the converts here. The dissenting Jews however, caused another division that resulted into assaults among the Jews and Gentiles. The apostles being privy to the plot to rough-handle and stone them, they immediately quit the town and fled to Lystra and Derbe cities.

At the first missionary journey, Paul also preached at Lystra where he healed a crippled man who had been lame from the mother's womb. The people were so amazed that the crowd attempted to worship Paul and Barnabas as deities. The evidence of miracles performed by the missionaries however, did not prevent persecution as people from Iconium came to dissuade the people until the apostles were stoned and drawn out of the city. They, in any case returned back to Antioch in Syria where he possibly wrote the epistle to Galatians. The sum of the Paul's first missionary journey is given below:

1. The team succeeded in making contacts in about ten notable cites including Seleucia, Salamis, Paphos, Pamphylia, Perga, Atelia, Antioch of Pisidia, Iconium, Lystra and Derbe.

2. the mission witnessed severe oppositions and Persecutions.

3. there were miracles, signs and wonders attesting to their ministries.

4. most of the cases of the persecution experienced came from the religious and Jewish leaders.

5. that persecution did not hinder the people from going back to visit the towns they were persecuted and stoned.

6. the pattern of the missionary activities laid the foundation for the need of effective follow-up of coverts

7. Paul established churches in South-East of Asia Minor.

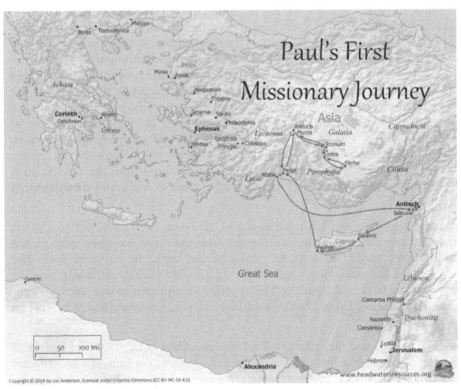

Paul's Second Missionary Journey 49-53 A.D. - Acts 15:39-18:22

Paul had a sharp disagreement with Barnabas on the issue of whether or not John Mark, who had left them during the first missionary trip should be allowed in their company again. Paul's opinion was to keep John Mark (who had left them on the mission field at Pamphylia) out of the second mission while Barnabas was in favor of John Mark being tolerated in the trip. So, due to the contention, Paul decided to go without both Barnabas and John Mark and chose to go with Silas (who replaced Barnabas) with the blessing of the church. The original intent of Paul's second mission was to revisit all places that they had planted churches to see the brethren, encourage them and give the decrees of the church that emerged from the council at Jerusalem. The journey that eventually covered 2,800 miles (4480 kilometers) started again from Antioch of Syria. This time, the team decided to pass through the region of Cilicia to Derbe and Lystra to confirm the spiritual state of the brethren. It was at Lystra that Timothy (who had both Jewish and Greek parentage) was recruited into the missionary team after Paul had circumcised him. They canvassed the territory of Galatia and Phrygia in Asia Minor and passed through Mysia to Troas. It was at Troas that Paul had the Macedonian call. Paul immediately left Troas for Samothrace and the next day Neapolis. This probably brought the first entrance of the gospel in present day Europe.

From Neapolis, they came to Philippi, one of the main cites of Macedonia where the missionary team spent some times. Some women including Lydia and her household from the city of Thyatira (who traded on purple) responded to the gospel. Here also, Paul had an encounter with a damsel possessed with the spirit of divination that led to their arrest and consequent imprisonment. The miraculous opening of the prison doors for Apostle Paul led to the conversion of the Philippian jailor who was instantly baptized. Paul was therefore unceremoniously released from prison.

From Philippi, Paul's team passed through Amphipolis to Thessalonica where they had a considerable number of converts added to the faith. Provoked by the huge success of Paul and Silas' ministry among the Gentiles here the unbelieving Jews stirred up an uproar against them. Paul and Silas escaped to Berea through the mercies of the brethren.

At Berea Paul and Silas also had an opened door as many Berea Greeks (both men and women) readily received the gospel. Again, the Jews from Thessalonica came to expel Apostle Paul from Berea leaving behind his missionary associates Timothy and Silas to continue the work a while.

The persecution at Berea drove Apostle Paul to the highly idolatrous city of Athens. In their superstitious belief the Athenians had raised an altar to the unknown God. At the sight of the magnitude of their idolatry and evident superstition, Apostle Paul's spirit was stirred up: he became indignant and grief stricken. According to Henrietta C. Mears, Apostle Paul preached a memorable sermon on Mars Hills. (Acts 17: 32). He had an encounter with the philosophers, Epicureans and Stoics who mocked at the gospel. Paul was arraigned before the court of Areopagus to defend the 'strange doctrine' in Athens. Paul did not have much fruits at Athens. Nevertheless, Dionysius the Areopagite, Damaris (a woman) and few others were the outstanding converts during his ministry at Athens.

Corinth is the municipal city and capital of Corinthians. Paul left Athens for Corinth where he came in contact with a certain Jew Aquila and his Priscilla. Aquila who had left Rome at the edict of Claudius that expelled all Jews from Rome. Aquila practiced the same profession of tent making with Apostle Paul. Note, Timothy and Silas from Macedonia joined him at Corinth. Again, Apostle Paul was gravely 89 opposed by the Jews in their synagogue at Corinth but they took refuge in the house of one Justus whose residence was very close to the synagogue. At Corinth, Crispus (the chief ruler of the synagogue believed the teachings of Paul. He embraced the Christian faith and was baptized. Encouraged by the vision he received, Paul spent eighteen months in Corinth despite the resistance and opposition of the Jews. Gallio the deputy of Achaia summarily dismissed the charges against Paul as he found no criminal offence in the charges against him. Paul left Corinth for Antioch via Syria in the company of Aquila and his wife (Priscila). At Ephesus he had occasion to preach the gospel in the synagogue of the Jews.

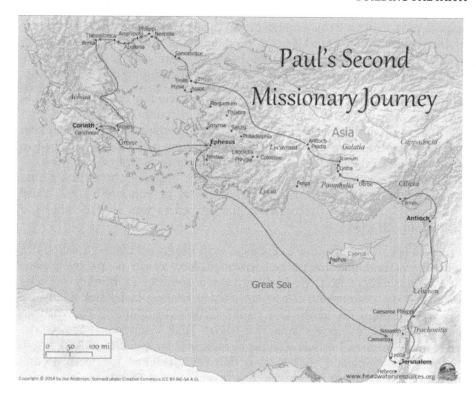

Paul's Third Missionary Journey 53-57 A.D. - Acts 18:23-21:17

After Paul had gone to give an update (in Antioch in Syria) of all that God did through him and his team during the second missionary outreach, he swiftly proceeded on the third missionary journey that was aimed at strengthening the disciples in the churches he had planted previously. Thus, he went through the regions of Galatia and Phrygia visiting the churches in Derbe, Lystria, Iconium and Antioch in Turkey which he had planted during his first missionary journey some five years ago, before departing to Ephesus. Before now, Paul in his second missionary journey had spent some quality time at Ephesus. But this time he had an encounter with twelve believers who had been instructed by Apollos (a Jewish believer born at Alexandria). These twelve disciples had evidently displayed that their knowledge and faith in Jesus was not more than what they had heard at the baptism of repentance by John the Baptist. In other words, these twelve believers were ignorant of the complete gospel of Jesus Christ. That is, they had not the understanding of the concept of salvation through the sacrifice of Christ. That is, they lacked the knowledge of being born again by faith in the atoning death of Jesus Christ. Neither had they the knowledge of the need for the experience of Spirit baptism. They were however, before now baptized in water by John the Baptist. Perceiving their gross deficiency in knowledge and Christian

31

experiences, Paul took them and baptized the in water again after instructing them in the way of the Lord Jesus. Consequently, he laid his hands on them to receive the Holy Spirit. And they (all the twelve) received the gift of the Holy Spirit with the evidence of speaking in tongues and prophesied (Acts 19:1-5).

Suffice it to note here that Paul's three months period in Ephesus: preaching and teaching in their synagogue was not without any resistance and opposition of some unbelievers. In short, due to the persistent perversion of the gospel message by some of the unbelievers in Ephesus, Paul had to withdraw himself with the disciples who were receptive to the truth, to the school premises of one Tyrannus, where he discipled them for a period of about two years. Nevertheless, his ministry at Ephesus (in this third missionary journey), as recorded in the scriptures was with notable and marvelous miracles.

Paul had become so popular in Ephesus with his gospel message, especially, with the marvelous miracles he performed. Most of the people in Ephesus heard the word of God. He had performed some extraordinary miracles including the casting out of evil spirits and healing many sick of diverse diseases through his apron and handkerchiefs. In addition, Paul had an encounter with the seven sons of a Jewish High Priest name Sceva, who were fake exorcists. In their attempt to replicate the miracles of Paul, began to use Paul's name and 'that of Jesus that Paul preached' for deceptive and fake exorcism. Unfortunately for the seven sons of Sceva, the evil spirit did not submit to their authority even though the spirit did acknowledge the authority in the name of Jesus and claimed to know Paul. Rather, the demonized person bounced on the seven sons of Sceva and prevailed on them until they fled away naked and wounded. This singular act in addition to other extraordinary miracles of Paul provoked much revered for the name of Jesus among the Ephesians to the extent that many others who were given to the practice of magic repented (Acts 19:13-19).

Paul's antennary was to continue his missionary trip before returning to Jerusalem and probably visit Rome later, to this end, he sent Timothy, and Erastus as his herald to Macedonia while he remained at Ephesus. Ironically, the works of Apostle Paul at Ephesus sparked a near riot and an uproar in the city as the Demetrius the silversmith began to incite the populace against Paul. It is an understatement to say that Paul's preaching and way of life, undoubtedly, had gravely posed a threat to their idolatrous way of life and means of livelihood hence, the concuss. With the intervention of the town clerk, Paul quietly bids the disciples at Ephesus farewell and departed to Macedonia not without writing the first Epistle to the Corinthians at Ephesus. While at Macedonia, in addition to visiting the churches in Philippi, Thessalonica, and Berea, he wrote the second epistle to the Corinthians before making his way to Corinth where he spent three months.

At Corinth, Paul had planned to go through Syria before he uncovered the unbelieving Jews' plot to ambush and assassinate him. He then changed his antennary and decided to return to Macedonia from where he had to retract his way back to Berea, Thessalonica and Philippi. At Philippi, he celebrates the Passover with Luke who later accompanied him to Troas where they were joined by other brethren from other churches on their way to deliver their palliatives at Jerusalem because of the famine. After about a week at Troas, the brethren had a night-vigil valedictory fellowship/communion service with Paul. At the service, the young man Eutychus fell asleep and fell from a window in a story building while listening to Paul's long farewell exhortation and died. But he was raised back to life. It goes without saying that this miracle was a great encouragement to the brethren in Troas.

From Troas Paul passed to Miletus via Assos. At Miletus, Paul sent for the elders at Ephesus who came to meet him for a word of encouragement and farewell. From there Paul and his missionary team departed to Tyre via Cos, Rhodes and Patara. On reaching Tyre, the brethren persuaded Paul not to go to Jerusalem. Their persuasion and that of prophet Agabus who had predicted that Paul would be bound and delivered into the hands of the Gentiles at Jerusalem fell on Paul's deaf ears. Paul insisted that he would go to Jerusalem and that he was not only ready to be bound but even to die at Jerusalem. Thus, Paul proceeded to Jerusalem without heeding the caution of the brethren. At Jerusalem however, as earlier predicted, Paul was arrested and imprisoned thereby terminating his third missionary journey of four years in about 57A.D. Source: Kurtz, J. H. Church History (Vol.1-3): Complete Edition (pp. 70-71). e-artnow. Kindle Edition. From Paul's third missionary journey we can learn:

1. That there is always the need for visitation and church strengthening mission of new churches planted in our contemporary times.

2. That often times, the different people used as instruments in the process of bringing others to the knowledge of salvation and for the perfecting of their faith in Christ are all significant as seen in the example of the church in Ephesus where we can possibly say: Apollos planted and Paul watered.

3. The experience of the sons of Sceva, depicted the futility of the efforts in using head knowledge

4. without experiential knowledge of the power in the name of Jesus.

5. The fact that those who previously used magical arts turned repented and turned to God showed that no one can be too bad, filthy or evil for salvation.

6. Paul's constant dependence on the leading of the Holy Spirit in his missionary outreaches is quite instructive.

7. The place of miracle as gospel advertiser and encouragement to believers is clearly brought out.

8. Paul commitment to obey God in the face of many persecutions is quite exemplary.

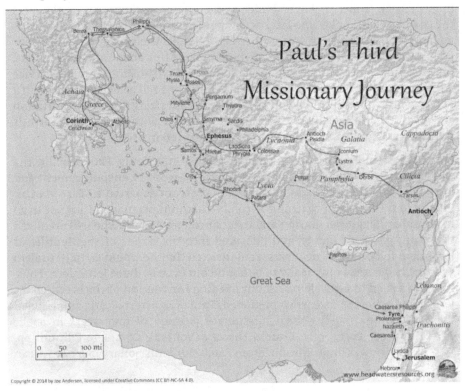

Undoubtedly, God was at work in the expansion and in the extraordinary spread of the Christian faith in the early church. In other words, there was a divine side in the expansion of the church, just as it is also appropriate to acknowledge the fact that God usually works with human hearts and hands. Several factors therefore contributed to the growth of the Early church in spite of the persecutions the church went through.

The Apostles

Peter

Peter was one of the foundational pillars of the early church leadership. He presided over the selection of Mathias to replace Judas from among the one hundred and twenty disciples in Jerusalem. He has been described as the 'Apostles to the Jews'. He spontaneously addressed the crowd to clarify that their Pentecost experience was scriptural. Along with John, they prayed for the lame man at the beautiful gate on their way to the Temple for prayers.

The Pentecost experience had produced a remarkable change in the man Peter, who had denied Christ three times. Peter turned out to be a bold proclaimer of Jesus to the whole world. He also boldly defended his faith in Christ before the high priest and the Sanhedrin who were amazed at the theological conviction and perception of the untrained apostles.

Peter, after having for some years held the office of bishop at Antioch, traveled to Rome and later became the first Bishop of Rome, holding the office until 67 A.D. Peter suffered martyrdom at the same time with Paul. His execution followed the burning of Rome in July 64 A.D. (when Emperor Nero blamed the Christians). Consequently, many Christians were executed. Peter was crucified upside down in the city of Rome. According to history, Peter had protested that he was not worthy to be crucified in the same way his master Jesus Christ was crucified. Constantine the Christian Emperor in Roman Empire (312- 337 A.D.) later initiated the building of St. Peter Basilica, that is today the largest Christian church in the world to mark the burial spot of Apostle Peter.

John

Soon after the death of Paul and Peter, John supposedly settled in Ephesus, and there, with the temporary break caused by his exile to Patmos (Revelation 1), he continued to preside over the church of Asia Minor down to the time of his death in the time of Trajan.

The tradition that under Nero, John, had been thrown into a vat of boiling oil, and we are told how he emptied a poisoned cup without suffering harm. Another story tells of the faithful pastoral care which the aged Apostle John took in a youth who had fallen so far as to become a bandit chief. In the extreme weakness John in old age, he had to be carried into the assemblies of the congregation, and with a feeble voice could only whisper, "Little children, love one another."

John, in his old age, was much troubled by false teachers, who had begun to corrupt the Gospel. These persons are called "heretics", and their doctrines are called "heresy" from a Greek word which means "to choose", because they chose to follow their own desires, instead of receiving the Gospel as the Apostles and the church taught it. Simon the sorcerer, who is mentioned in the eighth chapter of the Acts, is counted as the first heretic, and even in the time of the Apostles a number of others arose, such as Hymenaeus, Philetus, and Alexander, who are mentioned by Paul (1 Timothy 19; 2 Timothy 17).

These earliest heretics were mostly of the kind called Gnostics, -- a word which means that they pretended to be more knowing than ordinary Christians, and perhaps Paul may have meant them especially when he warned Timothy against "science" (or knowledge) "falsely so called" (1 Timothy 20). Their doctrines were a strange mixture of Jewish and heathen notions with Christianity; and it is curious that some of the very strangest of their opinions have been brought up again from time to time by people who thought they had found out something new, while they had only fallen into old errors, which had been condemned earlier by the church.

John lived to about the age of a hundred. He was at last so weak that he could not walk into the church; so, he was carried in, and used to say continually to his people, "Little children, love one another." Some of them, after a time, began to be tired of hearing this, and asked him why he repeated the words so often, and said nothing else to them. The Apostle answered, "Because it is the Lord's commandment, and if this be done it is enough."

James, the brother of Jesus

The name of James was shared by two of the twelve disciples of Jesus: James, the son of Zebedee and brother of John, who was put to death by the command of Herod Agrippa I. (Acts 12:2) about A.D. 44, and James, son of Alphaeus, about whom we have no further information. A third James, designated in Galatians, the brother of the Lord, was the leader of the church in Jerusalem.

Shortly before the destruction of Jerusalem, the Jews at the Passover having desired of him a testimony against Christ, and he having instead given a powerful testimony on His behalf, he was hurled down from a pinnacle of the temple, stoned, and at last, while praying for his enemies, slain by the blows of a fuller's club. According to Josephus, however, Ananus, the high priest, after the recall of the Proconsul Festus and before the arrival of his successor Albinus, along with other men hostile to James, hastily condemned him and had him stoned, about 63 A.D.

Of the other Apostles little is written. It is believed that Thomas preached in Parthia, Andrew in Scythia, and Bartholomew in India; while in later traditions Thomas is stated to be the Apostle of India. Philip exercised his ministry from Hierapolis in Phrygia to Asia Minor, and Barnabas, conducted his mission and suffered martyrdom in his native country of Cyprus. However, other writings make him the founder of the church of Milan. It is said that John Mark wrote his gospel at Rome.

The Didache – 95-99 A.D.

The Didache (The Lord's Teaching Through the Twelve Apostles to the Nations) is the oldest surviving Christian church order, probably written in Egypt or Syria at the end of the first century. It is considered to be a work of patristic literature from an unknown Apostolic Father. The Didache is essentially an early church manual, which addressed practical morality, the way church services and Christian life should be conducted, and a reminder of the immanent return of Jesus Christ to the world. It is considered a gathering of the teaching of the disciples or apostles that Jesus Christ selected, and is anonymously authored.

Some early Christian writers treated the *Didachē* as canonical, and Egyptian authors and compilers quoted it extensively in the 4th and 5th

Eusebius of Caesarea quoted it in his *Ecclesiastical History* (early 4th century), and it formed the basis of chapter 7 of the 4th-century *Apostolic Constitutions*, a collection of early Christian ecclesiastical law. It was known only through such references in early Christian works until a Greek manuscript of it, written in 1056, was discovered in Istanbul in 1873 by the metropolitan Philotheos Bryennios. He published it in 1883. Two fragments of the work were later discovered: a 4th-century Greek papyrus in Oxyrhynchus, Egypt, and a 5th-century Coptic papyrus in the British Museum.

The *Didachē* is not a unified and coherent work but a compilation of regulations that had acquired the force of law by usage in scattered Christian communities. Evidently several preexisting written sources were used and compiled.

Chapters 1–6 give ethical instruction concerning the two ways, of life and of death, and reflect an early Christian adaptation of a Jewish pattern of teaching in order to prepare catechumens (candidates for Christian baptism).

Chapters 7–15 discuss baptism, fasting, prayer, the Eucharist, how to receive and test traveling apostles and prophets, and the appointment of bishops and deacons.

Chapter 16 considers the signs of the Second Coming of the Lord. https://www.britannica.com/topic/Didache

The influence and importance of this document to its original readers and even to modern-day Christian believers is impressive. *The Didache* presents a clear and concise advice on dealing with the pragmatic constructs of the Christian church. However, it still cleverly and successfully melds the functionality of Christianity with its spiritual side.

Thus, the importance of The Didache should not be dismissed merely because of its size or exclusion from the Scriptures. Like many other theological works written at the time, its usage was at times questioned, and a general opinion of it emerged as it being non–canonical. Theologian and monk Tyrannius Rufinus (340–410 A.D.) specifically makes reference to The Didache and said that it would have been "read in the churches, but not appealed to for the confirmation of doctrine" (Schaff, 558). Athanasius of Alexandria (296–373 A.D.) states that this document was appointed by the Fathers to be read by those who newly join us, and who wish for instruction in the word of godliness. Eusebius Pamphilus, in his Ecclesiastical History, also speaks of The Didache as not being in the Canon of scripture. As such, it provides to the modern-day reader an understanding of the influence this work had on the early church despite its lack of canonical authority. It also shows that

Christianity, like the Jewish faith, had its own unique ceremonies of religious value.

The Didache provides direction on the public worship in the church and furnishes to its reader clear examples of how certain ceremonial activities are to be handled. For instance, its fourth chapter refers to daily prayer and states, "In church you shall confess your transgressions, and you shall not approach your prayer with an evil conscience." This gives to the reader a pragmatic but still personal call to prayer. Communication with God is important, but a pure heart is quintessential. Later on in its eighth chapter, the reader is urged to pray three times a day as Jesus did in Matthew 6:9-13. Again, this prayer should come from a clean heart free from hypocrisy.

Chapter 9 of The Didache offers three different prayers to be used specifically during the Eucharist (or Holy Communion as it is referred to today). One prayer is for celebrating the cup of wine which is Christ's blood, one is for celebrating the bread, which is Christ's body, and the last is a prayer of thankfulness for knowledge of Christ and for the future kingdom of God the Almighty soon to be issued into the world.

Besides specific instructions on what prayers are to be said during Communion, the reader of The Didache is also commanded, "Let no one eat or drink of your Eucharist except those who have been baptized into the name of the Lord." Unlike some "relaxed" communion services held today in various religious communities, The Didache directs this ceremony with exact purposes, provisions, and prohibitions.

Even more specific than the Eucharist, The Didache presents special rules on baptism. Certain ingredients must be present for this act to be legitimate to the Christian church: water of specific type and condition, personal preparation in the form of fasting and instruction, and correct theological phrasing on the state of the baptized. This creates a baptismal formula that is even used in modern times but has its origins in the Jewish faith. However, the Didache is not, of course concerned with Jewish rites of lustration but with the sacrament of baptism. The Jewish tradition is still influential, but in principle it has already been ruptured." The Didache sets up the distinctness of Christian baptism compared to Jewish practices and emphasizes the spirituality behind the act.

The Didache also touches on other miscellaneous liturgical practices such as tithing, fasting, fellowship and charity, and hospitality. In each of these, a generalized statement is made about what should be done, and then the writer of The Didache explains the reasons behind sponsoring such practices. For instance, it advises readers to give all the first fruits to the prophets or the poor, "in accordance with the commandment," and "Do not let your fasts coincide with those of the hypocrites," so fast instead on Wednesdays and Fridays. Additionally, believers ought to gather together for fellowship and perform acts of charity, "just as you find in the Gospel of our Lord." Moreover, they were to welcome everyone, "in accordance with the rule of the Gospel."

Whether speaking on the Eucharist, baptism, fasting or prayer, The Didache shows itself as a useful "manual of church order and practice." It offers a specific agenda or course of action to take as a church member in the body of Christ.

The Didache also focuses on the aspects of Christian morality and personal integrity and provides teaching on the two ways that a church member can take - one leading to life; the other, to death. Basically, in the era of Pax Romana, it shows the true pathways and roadblocks of Christian ethics.

This document points to Jesus and his teachings as to what constitutes a holy life. In its first chapter, The Didache promotes love for God and neighbor as a primary rule of living. The church members are called to deny themselves for God and humanity and to be sacrificially altruistic. Furthermore, church members are to live according to a number of moral rules - some right out of the Ten Commandments, but others (and this perhaps shows the Romanizing influence of the times) deal with sexual promiscuity of classical Greek or Roman culture. It is stated, "You shall not corrupt boys." As such, the Didache's commandments appear to be a more specific breakdown of the two Great Commandments.

Later the Didache pushes for a pure life and to "flee from evil of every kind, and from everything resembling it." As such, holiness, morality and high ethical standards are important. Although the majority of The Didache deals mainly with the rules -personal and public - of the early Christian, in chapter 16, it presents to its readers the necessity and purpose of these prescribed attitudes and practices.

It is crucial to understand the mindset of the early Christian church. There was an "eschatological sense of imminence" that Jesus would return to establish his kingdom. Therefore, it was essential that the early Christians maintain a holy life until the end. The Didache makes several eschatological references in the prayers offered earlier in chapters 8-10 such as "Your kingdom come" and "so may your church be gathered together."

The eschatological hope was that Christ's return was going to occur very quickly, so church leaders had to maintain a level of holiness in order to be found blameless. Although this hope had its origins in the New Testament, the leaders still considered The Didache "not 'canonical' but 'ecclesiastical'." Its usefulness as a church manual on practices and the catechumenate was important but, for theological purposes, its evaluations lacked the substantiation and spiritual depth of other books in the New Testament.

The Didache provided the early church with an instruction manual on how to deal with very complex issues, both in the personal and public arena.

Its brevity should by no means lessen its importance for many other works. The Didache aided a great number of people in the early church to focus, through liturgy and moral practice, on what it means to be a Christian. Faith was not just a feeling of spirituality; it required a great deal of effort and respect in its expression within the church and in the world. https://www.worldhistory.org/article/904/the-didache-a-moral-and-liturgical-document-of-ins/

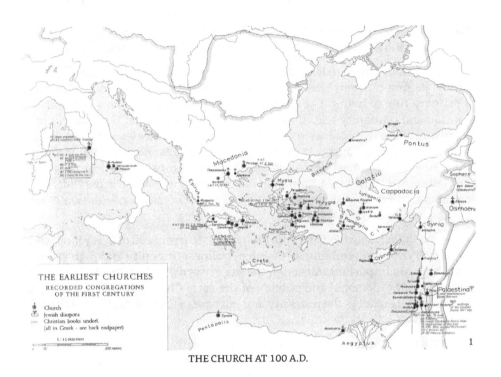

THE CHURCH AT 100 A.D.

THE GROWING CHURCH 100 – 300 A.D.

From the first century to the early fourth century, the church had passed through innumerable ordeals of both organized and unorganized persecutions. For over three hundred years the church suffered and was in danger of persecutions. The blood of the martyrs was then said to be the seed of the church. These persecutions were extremely painful but very fruitful as the church grew in the face of sufferings.

Christianity, as a Jewish sect had enjoyed initial protections under Roman's policy of freedom for local religions. But, as soon as the early believers came declaring that there was another King, they immediately incurred the wrath of the emperors who saw that as a threat to emperor worship.

Secondly, Christianity was totally incompatible to Rome's world view system: politically, socially, economically and religiously.

Thirdly, the persecutions were closely related to the political situation in the empire. The empire had become unstable, chaotic, with the decline in moral values. Hence, the consequent search for source of strength from existing establishments. It was considered necessary for religion to be united and in support of the state. The Roman Emperors therefore, demanded an outward agreement with paganistic religions. The Christians who were opposed to and resented pagan rites and practices became victims of more persecutions.

As Christianity developed in Israel, the Jewish leaders sought to snuff out the early church. These leaders went so far as to convince the Roman empire to persecute the Christians as well. The Romans at first were not eager to comply with these requests but eventually under Emperor Nero. In 64 A.D., a devastating fire broke out in the city of Rome. Nero resorted to accusing the Christians of causing the fire. He not only accused the Christians but also began the Roman persecutions on the Christians. These persecutions included mockery, torture, and death.

Other reasons for these persecutions were that the people of the Roman Empire misunderstood what Christianity was all about. They accused the Christians of various crimes, including black magic. For instance, the Christian Lord's Supper was misunderstood for cannibalism. Similarly, because the Christians would not participate in their public entertainments at their theatres and or in other worldly parties, they were regarded not only as anti-socials but as haters of mankind. In the same manner, many Christians who refused participation in military services incurred the wrath of the emperor as they were considered unpatriotic.

Economic issues were also a cause to these persecutions. For instance, the practice of idolatry was a common feature in the whole empire. It made the goldsmith or silver smith profession that produce various materials for idol worship a lucrative business. With the mass conversions of pagans to Christianity in the empire, some of these idol producing traders and craftsmen were fast losing their sources of income. Many Jews hated Christians because of their anti-Judaism practices. More importantly, the early church was persecuted for their refusal to worship the Roman gods. Those who would not worship the Roman gods were regarded as atheists. This was because every disaster was attributed to the disfavor of the gods. All efforts were therefore made to keep the gods happy in the empire. It was then considered a height of heinous crime for any Christian to refuse to worship these gods. An act that was tantamount to provoking the gods to wrath. Such was considered a great threat to the peace and stability of the whole society.

The Jews were gradually acquiring the attribute of being a hated race. Unfortunately, a number of the early Christians were of Jewish origin. Anti-Jewish feelings were vented on the Christians for their non-distinctive mixture of gentile and Jews in their assemblies.

However, when war broke out between Rome and Israel in 67 A.D., the persecutions lessened due to Rome being more focused on the war. In Domitian's (81-96 A.D.) reign many Christians were massacred and during Emperor Trajan (98-117 A.D.), Ignatius, Bishop of Antioch was thrown to the wild beasts in the colosseum at Rome in 115 A.D. Simon of Jerusalem who was the second Bishop of Jerusalem (63 –107 A.D.), was also tortured for many days and finally crucified in 107 A.D. The saintly Polycarp of Smyrna, who was a disciple of Apostle John was burnt at the stake in 155 A.D. under Emperor Antiochus Epiphanes. Under Marcus Aurelius (161 – 180 A.D.) the persecution continued for years and included the beheading of Justin Martyr, the apologist in Rome in 166 A.D. The persecution of the Christians and the church, predicted by Christ had begun during the Apostolic Era "Blessed are those who are persecuted because of righteousness, for theirs is the kingdom of heaven. Blessed are you when people insult you, persecute you and falsely say all kinds of evil against you because of me." (Matthew 5:10, 11). The blood of the Martyrs became the seed of the church.

As the blood of the saints dropped, it fertilized the harvest fields for the planting and germination of churches. There were no clear evidences or records of ever extinguishing the fire of the church through persecution in the early church. Rather persecution appeared to have fanned the fire of the surviving believers to be ablaze with enthusiasm for the defense of the truth and the spread of the gospel. It may be that the early church had very well understood that they that will live godly in Christ Jesus in his world shall suffer persecution (2 Timothy 3:12). No wonder, it has been noted that next to the righteousness of the early believers was the phenomenon of persecution which they faced expectantly. The faith of our fathers and the footsteps of uncompromising martyred heroes of faith may serve to encourage all persecuted churches, local assemblies and Christian groups and even individual believers.

In the face of overwhelming persecutions, the Christians remained faithful. The Christians were neither known to be bad neighbors nor disloyal as long as that did not contradict their beliefs. For instance, Apostle Peter was said to have exhorted his readers to submit to blood thirsty Emperor Nero the initiator of the first organized persecutions of the Christians.

Jerusalem after 100 A.D.

Before the destruction of Jerusalem in 70 A.D., many Christians had fled to the city of Pella, which is in modern day Jordan. Tradition holds that a Jewish-Christian sect of Nazoreans made their way to Pella and settled in the city which became a Jewish Christian hub during the early days of Christianity. The disciples had been miraculously told by Christ to abandon Jerusalem because of the siege it was about to undergo.

Pella is alleged to have been the site of one of Christianity's earliest churches, but no evidence has been found of this. According to historian Edward Gibbon, the early church of Jerusalem fled to Pella after the destruction of the temple in 70 A.D., staying there until their return during the reign of Emperor Hadrian, making it a secondary pilgrimage site for early Christians and modern Christians today.

After Jerusalem's destruction, many Jews also fled to Pella as well. Therefore, the headquarters of the Jerusalem church was actually in the city of Pella. Symeon was the Bishop of the Jerusalem church during the rule of Trianon (98-117 A.D.), but was accused for his apostolic zeal by the heretic Jews to the Consul Atticus, who arrested him and after terrible torture, condemned him to a crucifixion death. There were then twelve successors to Symeon from 107 A.D. to 134 A.D. due to continued persecutions.

Jerusalem was demoted to a mostly insignificant large village, built on the ruins of her glorious past. Despite all this, Christianity had spread throughout the whole of Palestine, while numerous Christian communities were created in different Greek urban centers such as: Caesaria of the Mediterranean, Ptolemaida, Joppe, Gaza, Bethlehem, Caesaria of Philipou, Scithiopolis, Neapolis, Neapolis, Pella, Gerasa, Vostra, Petra –and elsewhere. Gradually, while Judaism was significantly confined, Christianity held and continued to spread. With the influx of Greeks to this area, Hellenism also spread and strengthened throughout Palestine, so that the main element of the population of Palestine after the destruction of Jerusalem, was the colonizing by the Greeks. The soon restored church of Jerusalem was composed mostly by the Greeks from the church of Pella.

The Christians in order to erase every Jewish element, which also annoyed the Roman authority, would elect Bishops who were non-Jewish and mainly Greeks.

Despite the sad events that intervened following the destruction of Jerusalem by the Roman armies, the Holy Places were not forgotten by the Christians. On the contrary, they remained alive in their memory, they would visit them and surround them with respect and love until the time of emperor Hadrian (117-138 A.D.). Emperor Hadrian built a pagan temple in Jerusalem at the precise site of Jesus' crucifixion. Hadrian also prohibited the Jews to approach the Holy City. On Jerusalem's ruins he founded a new city, Aelia Capitolina. In fact, to obstruct the settlement of Christians in the Holy Places, he ordered that they be covered with earth and then built a statue of Zeus and Aphrodite on Golgotha. Jerusalem in her new state not only did not differ from the other Roman colonies, but it appeared inferior to them.

The Christians that were able to return to the Jerusalem area settled in Aelia and formed a cluster of Christian communities. During this period begins a new era in the history of the church of Jerusalem. The holy City was subject politically and administratively to Caesaria, the seat of the ruler of Palestine. Also, the jurisdiction of all the districts of the Holy Lands were borne by the Metropolis of Caesaria. Due to this the Bishop of Jerusalem was under the Bishop of Caesaria, who was over of all the District of Palestine. In the meantime, Hadrian had started to persecute not only the Jews but also the Christians. He in fact ordered that anything pertaining to Judaism or Christianity should disappear from Bethlehem and Jerusalem.

Later after Markos, Bishop of Jerusalem, Cassianos was elected. Later Narcissus the Wonderworker (185-211 A.D.) became the Bishop of Jerusalem and he became the most important Bishop of Jerusalem since Symeon. However, Narcissus having been falsely accused, fled to the desert where he remained for a long time. In his place Dios was elected in 211 A.D. but then was succeeded almost immediately by Herman and Gordian (211-212 A.D.). In the meantime, Narcissus returned to Jerusalem. The people persistently implored him to accept again the pastoral care of the church. He however refused not being able to serve due to old age. https://en.jerusalem-patriarchate.info/history/the-first-church/

The next successor was Alexander from Cappadocia (213-251 A.D.) who having arrived in Jerusalem on pilgrimage. As a Bishop, Alexander pastored the church successfully, created an important library in Jerusalem, built a school in which the famous Origen taught and helped significantly in the development of theological manuscripts. After James, the brother of the Lord, the first Bishop of Jerusalem, Alexander held the position of primacy for the first time in the history among the learned Bishops of the church and was the first one to build a library and a school. The continuous progress of the church of Jerusalem was again interrupted by the persecutions by Decius (250 A.D). https://atlantaserbs.com/learnmore/history/Jerusalem-church.htm

Internal Challenges to the Church

In the history of the early church, the second and third centuries were very crucial periods. This was the era when Christianity had external foes and a more deadly and subtler enemy within. Thus, while the church was battling to preserve its existence amidst the several Roman decrees, edicts and policies that were aimed at the extinction of the church, it had to also fight doggedly to preserve its orthodox doctrine and faith. As the Imperial Roman authorities persecuted adherents of the Christian faith, the definition of the orthodox Christianity of the infant church was also threatened by the legalistic and philosophic influences from Jewish and Greek converts respectively.

Early converts to Christianity were either from a Jewish background of salvation by works or from intellectual environment of Greek philosophy. The attempts by the Jewish converts to interpret and express Christianity in harmony with the legalistic demands of Jewish laws and traditions on the one hand resulted to heretical ideas that were alien to the orthodox theology of the infant church. Especially, as converts from Judaism they emphasized monotheistic religion. Similarly, the philosophical pagan Greeks thought to dress Christianity in pagan philosophies. The implication of all these was the attempts of the leadership of the church to redefine and develop the authentic tradition of the church that led to schisms and even the consequent emergence of heretical sects.

For example, the Ebionites were generally a Jewish-Christian sect. They were Judaizers who had thought to safeguard the monotheism and the deity of Christ under the leadership of Bar Kokhba between 132 A.D. and 135 A.D., who was holding tenaciously to the supremacy of Jewish law. The Ebonites believed that both the Jews and Gentiles were bound by the Law of Moses. The Ebionites taught that Jesus did not possess any unique status other than a mere son of Joseph who eventually acquired or attained a measure of divinity at baptism when the Holy Spirit descended on Him. They insisted on circumcision as a pre-requisite for salvation in addition to faith in Christ. The Ebionites extolled the gospel according to Matthew but had no regards for the writings of Paul. Their argument was that since Paul was not an eyewitness of Jesus, his authority was illegitimate. Ebionites were legalistic and frugal to the extent they saw poverty as a blessing.

Ebionite's also rejected the virgin birth of Jesus. Hence to them, Jesus was a natural son of Joseph and Mary. To them, Jesus is just a true prophet that was in accordance with Old Testament scripture (Deuteronomy 18:15-22). The Ebionites insisted that Jesus was a second Moses, a reformer and a teacher that perfectly fulfilled the law. To be converted to Christ, to the Ebionite, was to fully embrace the law of God and tradition of Moses. No wonder the Ebionites were renowned opponents of Marcionism. The influence of the teaching of the Ebionites began to abate after the destruction of Jerusalem even though there were still traces of them till 135 A.D.

Next the Gnostic sect challenged the Christian belief system. The word gnosis is derived from Greek meaning 'knowledge'. In church history, Gnosticism is a religious movement of the early Christian church that probably emerged in the first century but was denounced as heresy by church fathers. The Gnostics were followers of a variety of religious movements that posed the greatest philosophical threat in the early church. It was seen as a product of amalgamation of Christianity with Greek philosophy. Christian traditions have traced its origin to Simon (the Sorcerer) Magus (Acts 8). The Gnostics were therefore a variety of religious movements that stressed that people can obtain salvation through secret knowledge (gnosis) that was only accessible to its members. Gnosticism, though of pagan origin, shared common beliefs in apostolic Christianity: the need for salvation for man, the idea of the existence of a deity alongside with heavenly beings that are at work in the universe.

One of the fundamental beliefs of Gnostics is the principle of dualism. Every Gnostic believed that the world is ultimately divided between two cosmic forces of evil and good. In Greek philosophy, evil was associated with matter. Gnosticism therefore was an attempt to account for the problem of evil and human predicaments in the world. Gnostics have been described as one of the natural desires to create theodicy and give explanation of the origin of evil. Gnosticism is a philosophical system that was tended to proffer an alternative solution to the problem of evil but it eventually robs humanity of the responsibility of sin. Rather, they attempted to trace the origin of evil to before the fall. To the Gnostic the Creator God is wicked, evil and far removed from the Supreme Being that has no contact with the material world. The Gnostics disparage the world and all that belongs to it. To the Gnostics human beings do not essentially belong to the world but to a higher realm but trapped in a body. Hence the deliverance that man craves for is not from sin and death but from the imprisonment in the world. That man in this world is at the mercy of hostile powers that govern the seven heavens. Consequently, salvation is not through any redeemer or a Savior but by gnosis that supplies the knowledge of the truth about the true nature of man.

Finally, the Montanism sect named after its founder, Montanus, became another threat. Montanus was an enthusiastic young Christian and a self-proclaimed prophet of the second century in Phrygia, Western Asia Minor. Montanism emerged around 154 A.D. as an attempt of Montanus to bring the church out of formalism and the dependence on human leadership into a life of absolute dependence and guidance of the Holy Spirit. The church was born on the day of Pentecost: that signaled the fulfillment of the promised indwelling of the Holy Spirit (the Paraclete) in the church. Thus, Christianity started as a religion in which leaders depended on the leadership and guidance of the Holy Spirit (Acts 13:1-3). However, by the second century, the prominence of ecclesiastical bishops in the local assemblies emerged. As already discussed, the heresies of Marcion had led the church to the formulation and canonization of the New Testament scripture. Consequently, the church had agreed that all the inspired books were now written, as the word of God had been concluded. The result was that the church then depended on books more than the influence of the Holy Spirit. Thus, the enthusiasm and vitality that was characteristic feature of the early church, was by the second century giving way to ecclesiasticism. Spirit of prophecies gradually faded away from the church by the second half of the second century.

It was at such a time that Montanus rose up with a renewed emphasis on the Holy Spirit and eschatology to combat secularism, formalism and human organization of the church. Montanus became very fanatical in his emphasis on the Holy Spirit that together with two prophetesses: Prisca and Maximillia they all claimed to be the mouthpiece of the Holy Spirit (Paraclete) calling the church to a life of clear distinction between the church and the world. Montanus was a charismatic teacher that was able to command many followers that were attracted from among the poor of Asia Minor. His activities were concentrated in Pepuza and Tymion near Laodicea and Colossae where he thought to establish a prototype of the eschatological New Jerusalem. Montanism was generally called the New Prophesy: demanding a higher standard, greater discipline and sharper separation of the church from the world. Montanus believed that he and the two prophetesses (Prisca & Maximillia) were divine instruments for end-time revelation.

Montanism was a movement focused around prophecy, specifically the prophecies of the movement's founders which were believed to contain the Holy Spirit's revelation for the present age. Prophecy itself was not controversial within 2nd-century Christian communities. However, the New Prophecy departed from Church tradition. Montanus became beside himself, and being suddenly in a sort of frenzy and ecstasy, he raved, and began to babble and utter strange things, prophesying in a manner contrary to the constant custom of the Church handed down by tradition from the beginning. According to opponents, the Montanist prophets did not speak as messengers of God, but believed they became fully possessed by God and spoke as God.

A criticism of Montanism was that its followers claimed their revelation received directly from the Holy Spirit could supersede the authority of Jesus or Paul the Apostle or anyone else. In some of his prophecies, Montanus apparently, and somewhat like the oracles of the Greco-Roman world, spoke in the first person as God: "I am the Father and the Son and the Holy Spirit."

Many early Christians understood this to be Montanus claiming himself to be God. However, scholars agree that these words of Montanus exemplify the general practice of religious prophets to speak as the passive mouthpieces of the divine, and to claim divine inspiration (similar to modern prophets stating "Thus saith the Lord"). That practice occurred in Christian as well as in pagan circles with some degree of frequency.

In John's Gospel, Jesus promised to send the (Paraclete) or Holy Spirit, from which Montanists believed their prophets derived inspiration. In the Apocalypse, John was taken by an angel to the top of a mountain where he sees the New Jerusalem descend to earth. Montanus identified this mountain as being located in Phrygia near Pepuza.

In the face of falsity and heresies propelled by several heretical sects that threatened the orthodoxy of the Christian faith in the second century, there emerged Apologists, Polemists, and church Fathers (people like Irenaeus, Tertullian, Cyprian of Cartage, Augustine of Hippo and many others) who stood to defend the faith.

An attempt was made to show the falsity of heretical teachings. Irenaeus for instance, produced the first antagonistic work. Its approach was to describe vividly the Gnostic. To him, this is the best way to refute heresies. However, since the Gnostics had many secret teachings, it was difficult to describe them accurately. Similarly, the Montanism were exposed in different ways by examining the lives of the leaders. Alexander was one of the pioneering adherents, who was accused of robberies and arrested and later died in prison in 251 A.D., due to old age and was laid to rest in a modest tomb in the city.

The Orthodox church was challenged and was asked the basis for calling some groups heretics. That is, what gave it the authority to call the divisive Movements heretic? This led the early church clinging to only the materials that had apostolic origin. The standard they then used to determine documents were mainly three:

1. Apostolic Tradition: The Gnostics secret tradition was opposed to the deposit of faith handed down by the original apostles. Because of the several heretical writings in circulation, the early church insisted on apostolic deposit. These deposits were summarized into statements of faith known as creeds. This gave birth to what was later known as apostolic creed. Several denominations still recite the apostolic creed today.

2. Apostolic Succession: In an attempt to distinguish and weaken the authority of any heretical movement over the early church, the early church fathers resorted to apostolic succession as a measuring yardstick. Irenaeus and Tertullian and some others held that the succession of bishops stemming from apostolic lineage only would guarantee the unbroken handing on of apostolic doctrines. A list of apostolic successions was then drawn up for several churches. One of such lists that has survived till date is that of Rome.

3. The canon of the New Testament: With multiplicity of Gnostics gospel appearing in the mid-second century, it became necessary for the Orthodox church to define the authoritative writings. The criterion for selection was

apostolic authorship. The debates on what should constitute the canon of the New Testament however, continued till fourth century.

Early Apologist

The Apologists, generally were pagan converts who were well schooled in secular philosophy of their time before conversion. They sought to give rational justification for the Christian faith to the Roman Authorities who had severally misunderstood Christianity. These apologists used their knowledge of philosophy and literal skills to create a rational setting for Christianity (from the Old Testament perspective) as a superior religion to the Pagan practices of the Romans. The Apologists primarily based their arguments on the philosophy that, they were able to deduce from the Old Testament in their defense or explanation of Christianity. Succinctly put, the second century apologists were Christian writers who wrote to defend the Christian faith against false accusations and slanders of antagonists of the church. The true church was always destined to be misunderstood and slandered.

Justin Martyr was one of the most popular second century apologists. He had a pagan background but got converted to Christianity. Justin Martyr was born in Flavia Neapolis (present Nablus in Palestine). His quest for truth took him to several philosophical schools. He came across an old man in Ephesus who pointed out to him the futility of all philosophical thoughts, and then illustrated to him the scripture especially those that bore witness to Christ. Justin, who before his conversion had been impressed by Christian's moral attitude even in the face of death was converted. With zeal, he took the Christian faith into his philosophical schools. He grew to become a teacher in Ephesus and had Titian as one of his pupils.

Martyr wrote contentious works against the Marcionites and the Gnostics. Similarly, he wrote two apologies. His first apology was addressed to Emperor Antonius Pius (137–161 A.D.). The intent was to clear some prejudices and misunderstandings about Christianity. He insisted that the allegations that the Christians were atheists were not only false claims by the Pagan communities but unfounded. He argued that the Christians both in principles and practices do demonstrate higher standard of morality and sense of reasoning. The second apology was more of a passionate protest against injustices of the Roman citizens. He addressed it to the Roman Emperor toward the end of his life.

Justin Martyr's longest work was a dialogue with Trypho the Jew. It was aimed at refuting the Jewish objection to Christianity and proving the authenticity of Christianity from the Old Testament scriptures. Justin Martyr was himself later persecuted and was then executed together with some of his pupils in about 165 A.D.

Irenaeus (130 - 202 A.D.), the Bishop of Lyons with his disciple Hippolytus, stood out as the earliest theological voices and teachers. Irenaeus was born in Asia Minor about 130 A.D. He was a disciple of Polycarp of Smyrna who was himself a disciple of John the beloved disciple of Jesus Christ. From the Eastern part of the church in Asia Minor he left for the West as a missionary, particularly to Lyons in Gaul where he served as a Bishop until his death around 200 A.D. His major contributions were his five volumes "Against Heresies" written primarily to refute Gnosticism. His principal concern was the proclamation of the divinity of the Godhead while insisting on monotheistic character of the God of Christian religion. Irenaeus emphasized the incarnation of Christ as well as His redemptive attributes. Associated with Irenaeus was the controversy regarding the issue of Easter Victor, Bishop of Rome from 189-198 A.D. who excommunicated the churches of Asia Minor for not celebrating Easter on the Sunday after the fourteenth of the month of Nisan. Irenaeus defended theses churches of Asia Minor who observed this date and sanctioned Bishop Victor for his actions. Irenaeus was also noted for his opposition of the Montanists. Irenaeus' name was derived from a Greek word that means peace. He was said to have proved himself to be a peace maker in the paschal controversies. Irenaeus was a Bishop of Lyons in 177 A.D. whom early church tradition commended as a Martyr of the disturbance of 202 A.D.

The fundamentals of Irenaeus' write-ups included the affirmation of the threefold Godhead: The Father, Son and the Holy Spirit, according to the scripture. Irenaeus insisted on the unity of God in contradiction of the Gnostics demiurge. To Irenaeus, the world was created by one God, and that Jesus Christ the Son of the Creator God died to save mankind. Irenaeus believed in the bodily resurrection of the dead.

Clement and his pupil, Origen, were noted for their scholarship and favorable leadership role in theological thoughts in Greek school. They were the first and the greatest University Men in the early church. Their school was a center of philosophical and scientific learning as well as of theology. To the Alexandrian all knowledge had to contribute to the understanding of the truth which has its culmination in Christian theology. The Greek philosophical school of thought therefore, interpreted God and Christ by blending the philosophies of their day with the message of Christianity thereby producing Gnosticism.

Clement believed in the apostolic character of faith and its divine revelatory nature. However, he held that, philosophy supplemented but did not contradict the faith. To him, ignorance and falsehood is the greatest sin. Hence, God sent the Word into the world to reveal God so that man may attain immorality.

Clement (150-220 A.D.) was the first Christian scholar who thoroughly understood the Holy Scripture alongside with his vast knowledge of Greek philosophy. He understood the problems of the philosophical youths of his days who had encountered Christianity from the background of Gnostics' theory. Clement had to enter their world, disentangled their conception and slowly gave them the knowledge of Christianity. Clement lived and taught like a philosopher. The aim of Clement was clear. He wanted to be the Apostle to the Hellenistic intellectual world. His purpose and approach were more of pastoral than theological. That was why he labored and aimed not to win arguments, but to win men for Christ and to lead them on to salvation. Like the Gnostics, he brought Christianity into touch with the philosophies. To him, philosophy was a preparation for Christianity. Philosophy is a school master for the Greeks just as the law was a school master to the Jews.

Clement differed from Gnostics (who were not interested in the training of character) in his emphasis in Christian behavior. To Clement, spiritual insight comes from a pure heart to those who are humble enough to walk as a child with his father. Clement taught that God had implanted good seeds in all creation. He believed that Christians can learn from Greeks because all truth and goodness come from the creator. Clément's efforts were to find relevance in Greek thought for Christianity.

Within the church of the second and third centuries, there began to appear a difference in theological thought between the Greek churches and the Latin churches. Latin theology principally represented by Tertullian and his successor Cyprian both of Carthage in North Africa, tended to be more realistic and practical in their dealing with the issues of church and salvation. Tertullian was more pointed and hostile to Gnosticism and all philosophies that threatened the Christian faith.

Tertullian was the son of a pagan centurion of Carthage. He received his education as a pagan. He was converted from paganism in his thirties. Partially, because of his own personal abstinent conviction he broke away and joined the puritanical but orthodox charismatic sect of the Montanist about 207 A.D. He affirmed that the church of the apostle was the only true church that contains valid deposit of apostolic truth. He attacked the lukewarmness of the church.

Also, in his extensive writings were teachings on prayers, penance, patience, baptism and Trinitarian Christology. According to him, truth is found alone in the church which has been given the Bible. In his vigorous views of the law, he denied that capital sin could be forgiven after repentance. He upheld the messianic character of the Son and his atoning work. He majored on Paul's theme of sin and grace. Thus, he laid the foundations for the latter theology of that Great North African thinker: Augustine Bishop of Hippo.

Tertullian was not only from Carthage in North Africa but he lived most of his life in Carthage the capital of the Roman province of Africa. He was a trained lawyer from a pagan background. After his conversion he came back to Rome to serve. Tertullian eventually rose to the rank of a Presbyter at Carthage.

He was converted to Christianity in Rome in 196 A.D. Tertullian was one of the major Latin voices against the many theological teachings that seemed to pose a threat to the Christian orthodoxy in the second and third centuries. He detested and negated the moral laxities that were gaining prominence in the churches in Rome.

Tertullian was the first to use the term "Trinity" to describe the concept of the three persons in Godhead. Thus, he was a Trinitarian theologian. He was the first major Christian theologian to write and express his concepts in the Latin language. He was the Founder of the Latin theology. Tertullian used the term trinity to distinguish between the personalities of the Father from that of the Son. The statements 'the blood of the martyr is the seed of the church' and 'what has Athens to do with Jerusalem' were credited to Tertullian.

Tertullian was more interested in issues of salvation, sin, grace of God, church government, and doctrine relating to the church. He firmly projected the Messianic character of the Son (Jesus) and his atoning death. Tertullian was very rigid on his emphasis on the necessity for water baptism after repentance. He taught that sin committed after baptism was mortal that is not pardonable or forgivable. In any case he was opposed to infant baptism.

Tertullian also wrote five volumes against Marcion to defend the Christian use of the Old Testament books. To this end he emphasized the oneness of God (who is both Creator and the Savior). Similarly, he was against the 'New Prophecy' of the Montanism as he clearly claimed that the Holy Scriptures is the sole property of the church.

Origen (185 A.D.-254 A.D.), was a student of Clement. He took over the leadership mantle from Clement at the age of eighteen. He was a magnetic teacher who attracted students from many quarters even from hundreds of miles away. One of his earliest students was Gregory from Asia Minor. Origen saw philosophy far more than matters of idea but as a way of character formation. He therefore endeavored to instill in his students love for virtue. His students came to see their teacher as a model of a truly wise man. Origen produced six versions of the Old Testament titled Hexapla. He taught that the scriptures were the treasury of divine revelation which must be seen as a whole. In other words, if there was an apparent sense of a passage that contradict the necessary morality or nature of God, then there must be deeper lessons underneath the surface of the passage. He used much of the allegorical interpretation. He believed there are three levels of meanings in every Bible passage: the literal sense; the moral application to the soul and the allegorical or spiritual sense i.e. the mysteries of Christian faith. Origen believed that the Bible must be allowed to speak for itself. It must speak for God who inspired it. He did not allow the heretics to twist passages of the scripture to entrench some rigid and erroneous perpetrations. Hence, the whole Bible must speak to teach the central message of Christian truths. What would have happened to Christianity without the rationally interpreted Bible to field the mind and control the development of Christian thought? He saved the scripture for the early church and for all ages as a historical foundation of the Christian faith. He had a pioneering work on systematic theology. He was the first theologian to clearly define the whole intellectual framework of the Christian faith. He produced an unmodified work titled, 'the first principle' that was addressed to educated readers. He knew very well that if Christianity was to succeed in the age of shaping civilization, the Christian truths must be presented in a way that it must justify itself to the intellect as well as the hearts of mankind.

Origen was sometimes charged with heresies as he was always bold to speculate where the church had not definitely spoken. For instance, he taught that:

1. All creatures including the devils would one day be restored in communion with God.

2. Hell would be resurrected.

3. All these were rooted in his extreme emphases on the belief that God's love would eventually and someday triumph over the sinful and rebellious.

Suffice it to say that these assumptions and teachings deny the free will of man and its eternal consequences. Origen proposed as a doctrine that can only remain as a desire. Source: A History of the Early Church, (05 BC-AD 451), John A. Apeabu (Ph.D.). Department of Christian Religious Studies, Federal College of Education, Zaria. Ii, © 2020 John A. Apeabu (Ph. D)

In 250 A.D., Origen wrote his work, "Contra Celsum" which means "Against Celsum" countering the writings of Celsus, a pagan philosopher and controversialist who had written a scathing attack on Christianity in his work *The True Word*. Among a variety of other charges, Celsus had denounced many Christian doctrines as irrational and criticized Christians themselves as uneducated, deluded, unpatriotic, close-minded towards reason, and too accepting of sinners. He had accused Jesus of performing his miracles using black magic rather than actual divine powers. Celsus had warned that Christianity itself was drawing people away from traditional religion and claimed that its growth would lead to a collapse of traditional and conservative values.

Origen wrote *Contra Celsum* at the request of his patron, a wealthy Christian named Ambrose, who insisted that a Christian needed to write a response to Celsus. In the writing itself, which was aimed at an audience of people who were interested in Christianity but had not yet made the decision to convert, Origen responds to Celsus's arguments point-by-point from the perspective of a Plato like philosopher. After having questioned Celsus's credibility, Origen goes on to respond to Celsus's criticism with regard to the role of faith in Christianity, the identity of Jesus Christ, the allegorical interpretation of the Bible, and the relation between Christianity and traditional Greek religion.

Modern scholars note that Origen and Celsus actually agree on many points of doctrine, with both authors emphatically rejecting conventional notions of humanlike deities, idolatry, and religious literalism. *Contra Celsum* is considered to be one of the most important works of early Christian apologetics; the church historian Eusebius lauded it as an adequate rebuttal to all criticisms the church would ever face, and it continued to be cited throughout late antiquity. https://en.wikipedia.org/wiki/Contra_Celsum

Origen was singled out for attack in the persecution of Decius and died in 254 A.D.

Clement and Origen were aware of the meaning of salvation. They made possible the career of other great Christian leaders like Athanasius, Gregory of Nyssa and John Chrysostom. They demonstrated that the best of classical culture could find a home and future within the church.

Cyprian of Carthage (200-258 A.D.) was martyred by beheading on September 4, 258 A.D. He converted to Christianity at the age of 46, twelve years before his death. He rose to the post of Bishop of Carthage. He regarded the Roman bishops as primus inte-pares (first among equals). However, he resisted the attempt of bishop Steven of Rome to bring all the churches under his authority on the controversial subject of water baptism of heretics.

North African Christianity had produced many rigorous Christians who viewed martyrdom as ideal. Cyprian, who was born to a wealthy family became the bishop of Carthage in 248 A.D. after his conversion to Christianity in 246 A.D. Cyprian was a good example of the rigorous Christian life demonstrated by North African Christians in the early church. Cyprian's conversion experience, produced a remarkable change in his life. He asserted that: 'the new birth created in me a new man by means of the Spirit breathed from heaven.' Due to his commitment to chastity, he was a dedicated celibate as he was under the vow to remain single all his life. In addition, though he had a rich parentage, he chose to remain poor. To this end, in literal obedience to the scripture, Cyprian was said to have sold his luxurious estate and gave the money to the poor. Cyprian was so committed to his newly found faith in Christ that within the space of two years after his conversion he rose to the rank of a bishop. So, he was consecrated the bishop of Carthage in September 14, 248 A.D. Though, educated in rhetoric before his conversion, he would not read any literature other than the Bible and distinctively, Christian books. Cyprian was a skilled and a clear-headed administrator. Cyprian was opposed to Bishop Stephen's (the bishop of Rome) claim to supremacy over all other bishops. Cyprian taught that all bishops were equal just as the apostles were.

During the Decius' persecution of 250 A.D., Cyprian fled from the city of Carthage to hide but returned to the city in 251 A.D. When he returned the council of bishops met to stipulate conditions for re-admitting people who lapsed from faith. The stipulated conditions were however controversial issues for debates which later caused division of the church.

The main contribution of Cyprian to the church in third century was his most important work on: The Unity of the church in which he developed the Episcopal Catholicism. To Cyprian, everybody must be subject to the Bishops in order to be in the one universal church. In his writings Cyprian insisted that: Whosoever is he and whatever his character he is not a Christian who is not in the church of Christ.

There was no salvation outside the church. It is not possible for him to have God for his father who would not have the church for his mother. He who is not with the bishop is not in the church.

On the issue of whether or not Christian baptism could be received outside the Catholic church (that is, whether heretics could be baptized), Cyprian's stand was that the Spirit's gift of life and salvation were restricted to the Catholic church. To Cyprian, the ministers were to be seen as priests of the New Testament. The Lords Supper was to be taken as the sacrifice on the cross.

He regarded the Roman bishops as primus inter-pares (first among equals). Hence, he resisted the attempt of bishop Stephen of Rome to bring all bishops under his superior authority. It was later that the Roman bishop declared himself as the unchallengeable head of the Catholic church in the West.

Cyprian had much influence on the church in the West. He eventually died as a martyr: as he was beheaded in 258 A.D. https://www.havefunwithhistory.com/timeline-of-christian-denominations/

In the 2nd century, Christian thought and theology started to develop more formally. Various theological schools emerged, each with its own interpretations of Christian doctrine. For example, the Alexandrian School, based in Alexandria, Egypt, emphasized allegorical interpretation of Scripture, while the School of Antioch focused on a more literal interpretation.

Persecutions of the Christians continued during this entire period under various Roman emperors, such as Decius and Diocletian from 284-305 A.D. These persecutions were often localized but could be severe in some regions. They aimed to force Christians to renounce their faith or face imprisonment, torture, or execution.

Towards the end of the second century, Christianity was fast becoming a compelling movement that was penetrating into the main stream of the religions in the Roman Empire. More so that it had attracted the keenest minds of the day as adherents of Christ's teachings that were popularly known as followers of "the Way."

The Gospel spreaded significantly outside of the Roman Empire; and many Christian communities were established in the east.

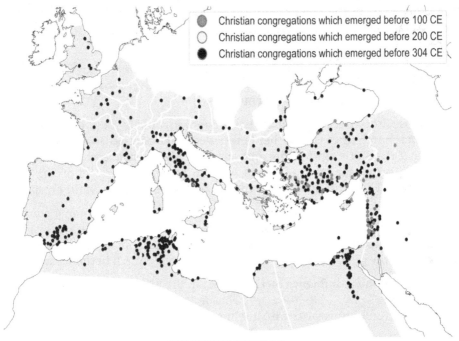

THE CHURCH AT 300 A.D.

THE CHRISTIAN EMPIRE 301 – 500 A.D.

Entering into the fourth century, Christianity had spread over most of Europe, North Africa, Asia Minor, and the Promised land. In fact, in 301 A.D. Armenia becomes the first country in the world to make Christianity its official state religion. Big changes were also happening in the Roman empire as Constantine rises to power in 306 A.D.

Constantine began his career by campaigning in the eastern provinces (against the Persians) before being recalled in the west (in 305 A.D.) to fight alongside his father in the province of Britannia. After his father's death in 306 A.D., Constantine was acclaimed as *Augustus* (emperor) by his army at Eboracum (York, England). He eventually emerged victorious in the civil wars against emperors Maxentius and Licinius to become the sole ruler of the Roman Empire by 324 A.D. Source: https://en.wikipedia.org/wiki/Augustus.

Upon his ascension, Constantine enacted numerous reforms to strengthen the empire. He restructured the government, separating civil and military authorities. To combat inflation, he introduced the solidus, a new gold coin that became the standard for Byzantine and European currencies for more than a thousand years. The Roman army was reorganized to consist of mobile units (*comitatenses*), often around the emperor, to serve on campaigns against external enemies or Roman rebels, and frontier-garrison troops (*limitanei*) which were capable of countering barbarian raids, but less and less capable, over time, of countering full-scale barbarian invasions. Constantine pursued successful campaigns against the tribes on the Roman frontiers—such as the Franks, the Alemanni, the Goths, and the Sarmatians and resettled territories abandoned by his predecessors during the Crisis of the Third Century with citizens of Roman culture. https://en.wikipedia.org/wiki/Constantine_the_Great

The Christian church faced another challenge with the Donatism sect in 312 A.D., leading to a schism in the church in the region of the church of Carthage, from the fourth to the sixth centuries. Donatists argued that Christian clergy must be faultless for their ministry to be effective and their prayers and sacraments to be valid. Donatism had its roots in the long-established Christian community of the Roman province Africa Proconsularis (present-day Tunisia, the northeast of Algeria, and the western coast of Libya) and Mauretania Tingitana (roughly with the northern part of present-day Morocco), in the persecutions of Christians under Diocletian. Named after the Berber Christian bishop Donatus Magnus, Donatism flourished during the fourth and fifth centuries. Donatism mainly spread among the indigenous Berber population, and Donatists were able to blend Christianity with many of the Berber local customs.

Constantine the first Roman emperor to convert to Christianity in 312 A.D. played a pivotal role in elevating the status of Christianity in Rome, decriminalizing Christian practice and ceasing Christian persecution in a period referred to as the Constantinian shift. This initiated the cessation of the established ancient Roman religion. Constantine is also the originator of the religio-political ideology known as Constantinianism, which epitomizes the unity of church and state, as opposed to separation of church and state. He founded the city of Constantinople and made it the capital of the Empire.

In 313 A.D. Emperor Constantine and Emperor Licinius, who controlled the Balkans, met in Mediolanum (modern-day Milan) and, among other things, agreed to change policies towards Christians following the edict of toleration issued by Emperor Galerius two years earlier in Serdica. The Edict of Milan gave Christianity legal status and a reprieve from persecution but did not make it the state church of the Roman Empire. This edict effectively legalized Christianity within the Roman Empire, ending the period of widespread persecutions. It allowed Christians to worship freely and restored confiscated church properties.

Emperor Constantine recognized the church as the one main hope for unity and stability within the Roman Empire. On the other hand, the church itself was torn by strife and dissension over Trinitarian and Christological controversies.

In 323 A.D. Eusebius completed his work "Ecclesiastical History"; the first major church history writing.

Council of Nicaea -325 A.D.

This was the first Post-Apostolic Ecumenical (world) Council of the church. It was at the instance of the First Pro-Christian Emperor Constantine. Soon after the cessation of persecution, the church found herself in a dilemma of defining the relationship between God the father and His Son Jesus Christ. On the one hand in the West, people like Tertullian had insisted on the co-equal, co-eternal, co-existence and co-substantial nature of the triune God (three persons in one God). Hence the evolution of the concept of Trinity which appeared to have negated the assumed 'Unitarian' concept of God by Judaizers.

The internal strife that began to rage did not allow the church to enjoy the external peace that ensued after Constantine's conversion. It all started with Arius of Alexandria who thought that the second person of the Godhead (Jesus Christ) is a creature. Athanasius vehemently opposed Arius teachings. Because of the threat posed by such a schism in the church to the entire Roman Empire, Emperor Constantine convened the first general Post-Apostolic Council of the church in May 325 A.D. at Nicaea, North West of Asia Minor. In attendance were not less than 318 Bishops of the whole church.

The decision of the council was that the teachings of Arius were condemned. It was decided that Arius and all his followers should be accursed. The council therefore created the "Nicene Creed" which states:

"We believe in one God, the Father, Almighty, Maker of all things visible and invisible; "And in one Lord Jesus Christ, the Son of God, begotten of the Father, only-begotten, that is, from the substances (ousios) of the Father; God from God, light from light, very God from very God, begotten not made, of one substance (homoousios), that is co-substantial with the father, through him all things are made, both in heaven and on earth; who for us men and for our salvation came down and was incarnate, was made man, flesh, suffered, and rose again. On the third day, ascended into heaven and is coming to judge the living and the dead; and in the Holy Spirit. "And those who say there was a time when he was not", and: Before he was begotten, he was not and: "He came into being from nothing" or those who pretend that the Son of God is "of another substance (hypostasis), or essence (ousia)" (then the Father) or "created" or "alterable" or "mutable", the catholic and apostolic church places under a curse" (Anathema).

The Nicene-Constantinopolitan Creed, often referred to simply as the Nicene Creed, has been a central statement of faith for both Eastern Orthodox and many Western Christian traditions.

Arius was banished with two others to Illyria. Two years later, the strife erupted again when the erratic Constantine accepted Arius back and banished Athanasius the Bishop of Alexandria who refused to reinstate Arius at the order of Constantine. In 326 A.D. Emperor Constantine orders the pagan temple in Jerusalem, built by Emperor Hadrian, to be destroyed and orders that the "Church of the Holy Sepulchre" be built on the same site, preserving the site of Jesus' crucifixion.

In 328 A.D. Athanasius writes his *The Incarnation*. To understand the importance of *The Incarnation*, it is important to put Athanasius in his historical context. Twenty-first-century Christians might be tempted to think that the doctrine of the Trinity was universally accepted in the early church. But much of the general body of theology we now take for granted, especially regarding the Trinity, had to be developed and worked out.

This popular belief supported by Arius stated that Jesus, though divine, was less than God. Arius taught that because Jesus was "begotten" by the Father, Jesus was a creature made by God; therefore, there must have been a point in time in which Jesus did not exist. The implications for this view were grave; if accepted, it would have meant that ultimately Christ's sacrifice on the cross would not have been sufficient payment for the sin of humankind. Athanasius was the prominent voice advocating for the divinity of Jesus. Not only was Athanasius a strong voice regarding the divinity of Jesus; he was also an important advocate for the doctrine of the Trinity over the course of his entire life.

Constantine was baptized by Arius on his death bed in 337 A.D. Athanasius however, remained to be known in the church as the father of orthodoxy. Shortly before his death, Constantine moved the capital of his empire to Byzantium and renamed it Constantinople (the modern-day city Istanbul) after himself. That meant that Rome had a rival city which further worsened the growing rivalry between the Greek churches and the Latin churches especially as he elevated the Bishop of Constantinople to a position equal to the Bishop of Rome. Consequently, this led to the division between Western and Eastern church i.e. between the Greek and the Latin churches. While it is true to say that the founding of Constantinople was not the cause of the rivalry but it however, provided a pivotal point for the rivalry groups.

During the reign of Constantine, an imperial decree established Sunday (Christian's day of rest and worship) as a day on which the people should not work. All legal businesses were forbidden on that day. This was later generalized sixty years later in the council of leaders.

Later in 367 A.D. Athanasius' Easter Letter confirmed the books of the Bible, and in 380 A.D. The Roman empire adopted them."

Council of Constantinople – 381 A.D.

The First Council of Constantinople, the second ecumenical council was held in May 381 A.D. in Constantinople. This time around, the council was summoned by Emperor Theodosius. The council was attended by 186 Bishops mostly Greek. The orthodox doctrine of the Nicene confession was affirmed but revised with the additional pronouncement that Christ was truly human as well as divine. This was necessary because after the Nicaea Council there appeared to have emerged the tendency of emphasizing the deity of Christ at the expense of his humanity. Similarly, the person and deity of the Holy Spirit were affirmed thus:

Holy Spirit who is the Lord and Giver of Life, who 'proceedeth from the father, who with the father and the Son together is worshipped and glorified and who spoke through the prophets."

The council deemed it necessary to formulate a clear doctrinal statement on the third person of the Godhead- the Holy Spirit adding:

"And we believe in the Holy Spirit, the Lord the giver of life, who proceeds from the Father and the Son, who spoke through the prophets; and the holy Catholic church. We look forward to the resurrection of the body and of the world to come."

The Creed also had additional an article about the church stating:

"One holy Catholic and Apostolic church'. We acknowledge one Baptism for the remission of sins (and) we look for the resurrection of the dead and life of the world to come, Amen."

The decision of the council included:

1. the reaffirmation of the condemnation of any form of Arianism and Macedonianism and Apollinananism, and

2. the Council accepted the Niceno-Constantinople Creed, to modify the original Nicaea Creed of AD 325,

3. the council renewed the legislation imposing upon the bishop the observation of diocesan and patriarchal limits,

4. the status of Constantinople, the Imperial Capital of the Empire in the East was given the prerogative of honor as the New Rome,

5. the council rejected the consecration of Maxims as the Bishop of Constantinople.

The council also gave the Bishop of Constantinople a standing second only to the Bishop of Rome.

The fourth century era was generally credited with what could be described as a long period of protracted theological, Christological and Trinitarian controversies in the early church. Indeed, with the conversion of Emperor Constantine to Christianity and the consequent cessation of persecution of Christians in the whole of the Roman Empire, a New Haven for the doctrinal debates aimed at forging a united and universally accepted Christian Creed and Dogma ensued. In other words, the cessation of the varied persecutions which could be best described as 'foes from without', pave way for another turbulent era of formulating creeds and doctrines, and resolving theological controversies in the church, between 313 A.D. and 451 A.D. Undoubtedly, the church needed to define her extraordinary concept of three persons in the Godhead (monotheism), as against the popular polytheism. The zeal to affirm the oneness of God on the one hand and to defend the Triune God, created conflicts that the church could not easily play down.

The Trinitarian controversy ensued resulting in different perceptions of God between Arius and Athanasius in the early church. This was as a result of the absence of a well-defined concept of trinity at that time. Many had conceived Jesus as the impersonal one that was not co-existent with the Father, while the other yet saw Jesus as a personality who shared the same essence with the father and co-eternal with the Father but subordinate to the Father. At this time, the person of the Holy Spirit was rarely mentioned in the discussions and debates.

The belief in monotheism, that is: The Lord our God is one God remained one of the uncompromised tenets of Judaism that was inherited by the Christian faith. However, Christians' insistence on the Lordship of Christ and the consequent worship of Christ while claiming the oneness of God somehow ignited questions of whether or not Christianity is a religion of two gods. The influence of Monarchianism (that was out to defend monotheism) with its emphasis on the denial of the Trinity was problematic. It was at this point that people like Tertullian and Hippolytus came out clearly to oppose the Monarchianism's concept of the Godhead in the west. Origen in the east, similarly affirmed the trinitarian concept as expressed in the Apostolic Creed. Although Origen may rightly take the credit of being the first church Father to explain the relationship of the Father to the Son as that of eternal generation but he however subordinated the Son to the Father. Hence, Origen's defense of the doctrine of the trinity has been described as the stepping stone for Arius heresy.

Council of Rome - 382 A.D.

The earliest known complete list of the 27 books of the New Testament is found in a letter written by Athanasius dated to 367 AD. The 27-book New Testament was first formally canonized during the councils of Hippo (393 A.D.) and Carthage (397 A.D.) in North Africa. Pope Innocent I ratified the same canon in 405 A.D., but it is probable that a Council in Rome in 382 A.D. under Pope Damasus I gave the same list first. These councils also provided the canon of the Old Testament, which included the deuterocanonical books.

The word canon comes from the Greek word meaning "a measuring" or "a rule." This is the word given by the early church fathers to those first apostolic writings, that alone, could be the "measuring rod" or rule to evaluate all scriptures. Acceptance of the Old Testament books as the rule and norm of faith was general in the early church. The varying acceptance or rejection of the apocrypha was not a problem until the fourth century. It was the fixing of the New Testament that was a major task for the early church. In the face of certain circulating Gnostic gospels and epistles, Irenaeus insisted that the test of validity of any inspired writing was whether it was written by the Apostles or by men closely connected with them. These writings: the New Testament, were considered equal to the Old Testament in regard to divine inspiration. Already in about 100 A.D. the thirteen letters of Paul had been collected and by the year 192 A.D., the term New Testament was already in use. By about 200 A.D. the western Christendom had recognized a New Testament canon which included Matthew, Mark, Luke, John, Acts, 1st and 2nd Corinthians, Ephesians, Romans, Philemon, Titus, 1st and 2nd Timothy, 1st and 2nd Thessalonians, Jude, Philippians, Colossians, Galatians, 1st, 2nd and 3rd John, Revelation and Peter's epistles of apocalypse.

Thus, the development of the New Testament canon into its final form as we now have it could not be until at earliest the second century in the Latin branch of the church. In other words, formation of the New Testament canon of the scripture and the apostolic creed came about at the same time. It is important to note that the creed was not written by the apostles. But it embodied the apostles' doctrine. This would lead to the baptismal confession for new converts later.

Council of Ephesus – 431 A.D.

The discussion of the Trinitarian controversy at the Council of Nicaea had triggered many debates on the relationship between the human and divine natures of Christ. The schools of theological thought in Alexandria and Antioch were divided on this issue with Alexandria laying more emphasis on the deity of Christ and Antioch on the humanity of Christ at the expense of his deity.

A typical instance of this was Apollinarius Christology. Apollinarius had taught that Christ had true body and soul but the Spirit was replaced with the divine "Logos" that dominated the passive body and soul in the person of Christ. Apollinarius projected the deity of Christ at the expense of His true human nature. On the other hand, Nestorius who was one of the popular theologians in Antioch before he was made bishop of Constantinople by Theodosius II had developed a teaching on Christology in Antioch that rejected the use of the title Theotokes (the mother of God) for the Virgin Mary. On his consecration as the Bishop of Constantinople, Nestorius found out that, what he had always taught in Antioch was opposed by the church of Constantinople. He emphasized the dual nature of Christ and suggested that theotokes be replaced with "Christotokos" (Christ bearer). This was his attempt to answer the question of: How can Jesus Christ be a man and not be a sinner since all humans are sinners by nature since the fall of Adam. Nestorius therefore taught that the incarnate Jesus was given birth by Mary and the divine Holy Spirit that is eternal and existed before Mary. He insisted that on the union of human and divine natures that Christ: is fully God and fully man.

Council of Chalcedon – 451 A.D.

This was the Fourth ecumenical Council of the church that took place 451 A.D. The council made a very significant contribution in the definition of the church's orthodox statement on Christology. Emperor Mercian had convened the Council of Chalcedon to affirm the dual nature of Christ, thereby rejecting the teaching of a single nature of Jesus Christ. In 444 A.D. Eutyches, one of the elderly monks of Constantinople, had begun to teach that there was only one "physic" (Nature in the incarnated Christ). Thus, Eutyches had denied that Christ had human nature. He insisted that Jesus had one single nature that was Divine. He blurred together two natures.

Eutychian believed in the fusion of the two natures (the divine and the human) in such a way that the humanity of Christ was completely absolved in His divine nature. In other words, the human nature was assimilated in the divine. The implication of this was that, according to Eutychian, the human body of Christ was different from our normal natural human bodies. This view was rejected at the Council of Constantinople in 448 A.D., not without an appeal to Leo the then Bishop of Rome. The dispute ended up with the proposition of a Christology as follows; that:

1. there were two natures (which are permanently distinct) in one personality,

2. the two natures (divine and human were united in one Person with each one performing its own proper function in the incarnate life,

3. from the unity of the divine personality and human personality follows the communication,

4. the work of redemption requires that a Mediator that is both divine and human, possible and impassable, mortal and immortal,

5. the incarnation was an act of condescension on the part of God but that in it the Logos did not cease to be the very God, and

6. the manhood of Christ is permanent. Thus, an inference to the rejection of the Docetism (i.e. the denial of the reality of the suffering).

It was at this Council of Chalcedon that the definition of Jesus Christ's dual nature was clearly defined as the Orthodox belief of the church. Thus, it brought the universal church's acceptance of the teaching that:

"Christ is the same perfect in Godhead and also perfect in Manhood; truly

God and truly Man." He is consubstantial (homoousios) with the Father oaring to the Godhead and consubstantial with us according to the Manhood. Jesus was therefore to be acknowledged in two natures in confusedly, "unchangeably", "indivisibly", and "inseparably."

The implication was that the Council maintained the distinction in the divine and human natures of Christ and yet united in one person. The co-existence of the two natures of Christ was known as hypostatic union.

The Chalcedonian Christology and Creed

After much debate on the dual natures of the one person of Christ, it was at the Ecumenical Council of Chalcedon that a final orthodox stand was taken. The orthodox definition of Christology that was formulated at Chalcedon meant the utter defeat and condemnation of Eutyches and all the adherents of his teachings of Monophysite in 451 A.D. The decision and the consequent Chalcedonian Creed formulated was:

"We following the holy Fathers all with one consent teach men to confess and one and same Son our Lord Jesus Christ The same perfect in Godhead and also perfect in manhood; truly God and also truly man, of reasonable soul and body; consubstantial with the Father according to Godhead and consubstantial with us according to manhood; in all things like unto us without sin; begotten before all ages of the Father according to Godhead and in these last days, for us and for our salvation born of virgin Mary, the Mother of God according to manhood one and the same Christ, Son, Lord, Only-begotten, to be acknowledged in two natures, in-confusedly, unchangeably, indivisibly inseparably, the distinction of nature's being by no means taken away by the union but rather the proper being of each nature being preserved and assuming one person and in one substance, not parted or divided into two persons but one and the same Son the Only-begotten, God the Word, the Lord Jesus Christ; as the prophets from beginning have declared concerning Him, and the Lord Jesus Christ Himself has taught us and the creed of the Only Fathers has handed down to us."

Ancient Era to the Early Middle Ages 501-1054 A.D.

Second Council of Constantinople – 553 A.D.

The Second Council of Constantinople is the fifth of the first seven ecumenical councils recognized by both the Eastern Orthodox church and the Catholic church. It is also recognized by the Old Catholics (Western Christians who separated from the Roman Catholic Church), and others. Constantinople II was convoked by the Byzantine Emperor Justinian I under the presidency of the Patriarch Eutychius of Constantinople. Participants were overwhelmingly Eastern bishops—only sixteen Western bishops were present, including nine from Illyricum and seven from Africa, but none from Italy—out of the 152 total.

The Second Council of Constantinople was the last phase of the attempt by Emperor Justinian I to ease tensions in the East with the remnants of the Monophysite movement, which was declared heretical at the Council of Chalcedon in 451 A.D. over the question of whether Christ had "one nature" (the Monophysite position) or two (the "orthodox" position).

At the end of 543 A.D. or the beginning of 544 A.D., Justinian issued an edict in which the supposedly Nestorian Three Chapters were officially condemned. His aim was to encourage the Miaphysites—the more moderate faction who insisted on "one nature" in Christ, to accept the decisions of the Council of Chalcedon and end the strife that had long plagued the empire over this issue.

The main work of the council was to confirm the condemnation issued by edict in 551 A.D. by the Emperor Justinian against the Three Chapters. These were the Christological writings and ultimately the person of Theodore of Mopsuestia who died 428 A.D., certain writings against Cyril of Alexandria's Twelve Anathemas accepted at the Council of Ephesus, written by Theodoret of Cyrrhus who died around 466 A.D., and a letter written against Cyrillianism and the Ephesian Council by Ibas of Edessa who died in 457 A.D.

The purpose of the condemnation was to make plain that the Great church, which followed a Chalcedonian creed, was firmly opposed to Nestorianism as supported by the Antiochene school which had either assisted Nestorius or had inspired the teaching for which he was accursed and exiled. The council also condemned the teaching that Mary could not be rightly called the mother of God (Greek: Theotokos) but only the mother of the man (anthropotokos) or the mother of Christ (Christotokos).

The Second Council of Constantinople is also considered as one of the many attempts by Byzantine Emperors to bring peace in the empire between the Chalcedonian and Monophysite factions of the church which had been in continuous conflict since the times of the Council of Ephesus in 431 A.D.

The bishops signed the canons condemning Origenism before the council formally opened. This condemnation was confirmed by Pope Vigilius and the third Council of Constantinople gave its "assent" in its Definition of Faith to the five previous synods. Also, one of the Acts of the Council at Constantinople, were the censures issued against those who rejected the Perpetual Virginity of Mary. https://en.wikipedia.org/wiki/Second_Council_of_Constantinople.

Justinian hoped that this would contribute to a reunion between the Chalcedonians and Monophysites in the eastern provinces of the Empire. Various attempts at reconciliation between these parties within the Byzantine Empire were made by many emperors over the four centuries following the Council of Ephesus, none of them successful. These propositions assert that Christ possessed no human energy but only a divine function and that Christ possessed no human will but only a divine will, "will" being understood to mean the desires and appetites in accord with the nature (promulgated in 638 A.D. by the same and opposed most notably by Maximus the Confessor). https://www.newworldencyclopedia.org/entry/Second_Council_of_Constantinople

The council also set forth its own eleven "chapters:"

1. If anyone shall not confess that the nature or essence of the Father, of the Son, and of the Holy Ghost is one, as also the force and the power; a consubstantial Trinity, one Godhead to be worshiped in three subsistence's or Persons: Let him be anathema...

2. If anyone shall not confess that the Word of God has two nativities, the one from all eternity of the Father... the other in these last days, coming down from heaven and being made flesh of the holy and glorious Mary, Mother of God... let him be anathema.

3. If anyone shall say that the wonder-working Word of God is one [Person] and the Christ that suffered another... let him be anathema...

4. If anyone shall say that the union of the Word of God to man was only according to grace or energy... as says the senseless Theodorus, or... (as says Nestorius) of two persons... let him be anathema...

5. If anyone... attempts thus to introduce into the mystery of Christ two hypostases... (or) if anyone shall calumniate the holy Council of Chalcedon, pretending that it made use of this expression ["two natures"] in this impious sense... let him be anathema...

6. If anyone shall not call... Mary the Mother of God... believing that she birthed only a simple man and that God the word was not incarnate of her... let him be anathema...

7. If anyone using the expression, "in two natures" ...so as to designate by

that expression a difference of the natures of which an ineffable union is unconfinedly made... let him be anathema.

8. If anyone uses the expression "of two natures" ...and shall not so understand... that of the divine and human nature there was made a hypostatic union... let him be anathema...

9. If anyone shall take the expression, "Christ ought to be worshiped in his two natures," in the sense that he wishes to introduce thus two adorations... let him be anathema...

10. If anyone does not confess that our Lord Jesus Christ, who was crucified in the flesh, is true God and the Lord of Glory and one of the Holy Trinity: Let him be anathema...

11. If anyone does not anathematize Arius, Eunomius, Macedonius, Apollinaris, Nestorius, Eutyches, and Origen, as well as their impious writings... let him be anathema.

In the seventh session of the council Justinian caused the name of Vigilius to be stricken from the diptychs. While Vigilius remained uncooperative for the present, the decisions of the council were quickly enforced throughout the East, and those who refused to endorse the council were removed from their posts and banished. The hoped-for reconciliation of the Monophysites and Chalcedonians, however, did not follow.

The Byzantine–Sasanian War of 602–628 A.D.

This conflict was between the Byzantine Empire and the Persian Sasanian Empire and it is also known as the Roman–Sasanian War, which marked the final and most devastating war in a series of conflicts between these two mighty empires. Here are some key points about this historical event:

The previous war between the Byzantine Empire and the Sasanian Empire had ended in 591 A.D. after Emperor Maurice helped the Sasanian king Khosrow II regain his throne. However, in 602 A.D., Emperor Maurice was murdered by his political rival, Phocas. Khosrow II declared war, apparently to avenge Maurice's death.

The war spanned several decades (from 602 to 628 A.D.) and was fought across various regions: Egypt, the Middle East, Mesopotamia, the Caucasus, Anatolia, Armenia, and even before the walls of Constantinople itself. The Persians initially achieved significant success, conquering much of the Middle East, Egypt, several Aegean Sea islands, and parts of Anatolia.

In 610 A.D., Emperor Heraclius came to power, and despite initial setbacks, he managed to restore a status quo. Heraclius's campaigns in Iranian lands from 622 to 626 A.D. forced the Persians onto the defensive, allowing the Byzantine forces to regain momentum.

The Persians made a final attempt to take Constantinople in 626 A.D., but they were defeated. In 627 A.D., Heraclius invaded the heartland of Persia, and a civil war broke out within the Sasanian Empire. The Persians eventually killed their king and sued for peace.

By the end of the conflict, both sides had exhausted their resources and achieved very little. Shortly after the war concluded, the Islamic Rashidun Caliphate emerged as the major political power of Persia. This war, often referred to as "The Last Great War of Antiquity," left a lasting impact on the region and paved the way for significant historical changes.

Arab-Byzantine War, 629-644 A.D.

Islam appeared on the scene amidst the change in society and economics in the Arabian Peninsula during the early seventh century. The adherents of the new religion immediately launched a campaign against the Byzantine Empire, the military, cultural and economic superpower of the age. In the course of just a few years the Arabs had conquered the valuable territories of modern-day Palestine, Syria, Jordan and Lebanon from the Byzantines. This was the first encounter between Islamic and Christian people and the aftermath set the stage for the Islamic conquest of North Africa, the Crusades and many other historical conflicts. The question "Why did the Byzantine Empire fail in the defense of these territories?"

The conclusion is that the Byzantines failed to recognize and address the great social changes that were taking place in the contested region while the Arabs expertly exploited the dynamic situation. The mighty Byzantine war machine had been devastated and imperial forces driven from Egypt, Syria and Mesopotamia by a small army of desert barbarians. The book industry in Alexandria was destroyed. The True Cross was in the hands of non-believers. The Muslims were building a new capital in Damascus and a new temple in Jerusalem while the Byzantines were fighting a last-ditch guerilla war in their homelands.

According to Muslim biographies, Muhammed, having received intelligence that Byzantine forces were concentrating in northern Arabia with intentions of invading Arabia, led a Muslim army north to Tabuk in present-day northwestern Saudi Arabia, with the intention of pre-emptively engaging the Byzantine army, however, the Byzantine army had retreated beforehand. Though it was not a battle in the typical sense, nevertheless the event represented the first Arab encounter against the Byzantines. It did not, however, lead immediately to a military confrontation.

There is no contemporary Byzantine account of the Tabuk expedition, and many of the details come from much later Muslim sources. It has been argued that there is in one Byzantine source possibly referencing the Battle of Mu´tah traditionally dated 629 A.D., but this is not certain. The first engagements may have started as conflicts with the Arab client states of the Byzantine and Sassanid empires: the Ghassanids and the Lakhmids of Al-Hirah. In any case, Muslim Arabs after 634 A.D. certainly pursued a full-blown offensive against both empires, resulting in the conquest of the Middle East, Egypt and Persia for Islam. The most successful Arab generals were Khalid ibn al-Walid and 'Amr ibn al-'As.

In the Middle East, the invading Rashidun army were engaged by a Byzantine army composed of imperial troops as well as local levies. According to Islamic historians, Monophysites and Jews throughout Syria welcomed the Arabs as liberators, as they were discontented with the rule of the Byzantines.

The Roman Emperor Heraclius had fallen ill and was unable to personally lead his armies to resist the Arab conquests of Syria and Roman Palestine in 634 A.D. In a battle fought near Ajnadayn in the summer of 634 A.D., the Rashidun Caliphate army achieved a decisive victory. After their victory at the Fahl, Muslim forces conquered Damascus in 634 A.D. under the command of Khalid ibn al-Walid. The Byzantine response involved the collection and dispatch of the maximum number of available troops under major commanders, including Theodore Trithyrius and the Armenian general Vahan, to eject the Muslims from their newly won territories.

At the Battle of Yarmouk in 636 A.D., however, the Muslims, having studied the ground in detail, lured the Byzantines into a pitched battle, which the Byzantines usually avoided, and into a series of costly assaults, before turning the deep valleys and cliffs into a catastrophic death-trap. Heraclius' farewell exclamation (according to the 9th-century historian Al-Baladhuri) while departing Antioch for Constantinople, is expressive of his disappointment:

"Peace unto thee, O Syria, and what an excellent country this is for the enemy!

The impact of Syria's loss on the Byzantines after the fall of Syria inspired continued invading and plundering of the entire territory of the Romans. In April 637 A.D. the Arabs, after a long siege, captured Jerusalem, which was surrendered by Patriarch Sophronius. In the summer of 637 A.D., the Muslims conquered Gaza, and, during the same period, the Byzantine authorities in Egypt and Mesopotamia purchased an expensive truce, which lasted three years for Egypt and one year for Mesopotamia. Antioch fell to the Muslim armies in late 637 A.D., and by then the Muslims occupied the whole of northern Syria, except for upper Mesopotamia, which they granted a one-year truce.

At the expiration of this truce in 638–639 A.D., the Arabs overran Byzantine

Mesopotamia and Byzantine Armenia, and terminated the conquest of Palestine by storming Caesarea Maritima and effecting their final capture of Ascalon. In December 639 A.D., the Muslims departed from Palestine to invade Egypt in early 640 A.D.

By the time Heraclius died, much of Egypt had been lost, and by 637–638 A.D. the whole of Syria was in the hands of the armies of Islam. With 3,500–4,000 troops under his command, 'Amr ibn al-A' first crossed into Egypt from Palestine at the end of 639 A.D. or the beginning of 640 A.D. He was progressively joined by further reinforcements, notably 12,000 soldiers by Zubayr ibn al-Awwam. 'Amr first besieged and conquered the Babylon Fortress, and then attacked Alexandria. The Byzantines, divided and shocked by the sudden loss of so much territory, agreed to give up the city in September 642 A.D. The fall of Alexandria extinguished Byzantine rule in Egypt, and allowed the Muslims to continue their military expansion into North Africa; between 643 and 644 A.D. 'Amr completed the conquest of Cyrenaica. Uthman succeeded Caliph Umar after his death.

The Byzantine navy briefly won back Alexandria in 645 A.D., but lost it again in 646 A.D. shortly after the Battle of Nikiou. The Islamic forces raided Sicily in 652 A.D., while Cyprus and Crete were captured in 653 A.D. https://www.medievalists.net/2012/06/arab-byzantine-war-629-644-ad/

Continued Hostilities

In 647 A.D., a Rashidun-Arab army led by Abdallah ibn al-Sa'ad invaded the Byzantine territory of Africa. Tripolitania was conquered, followed by Sufetula, 150 miles (240 km) south of Carthage, and the governor and self-proclaimed Emperor of Africa Gregory was killed. Abdallah's booty-laden force returned to Egypt in 648 A.D. after Gregory's successor, Gennadius, promised them an annual tribute of some 300,000 nomismata.

As the first tide of the Muslim conquests in the Near East ebbed off, and a semi-permanent border between the two powers was established leaving Syria in Muslim control and the Anatolian plateau in Byzantine hands. Both Emperor Heraclius and the Caliph 'Umar (634–644 A.D.) pursued a strategy of destruction within this zone, trying to transform it into an effective barrier between the two realms.

Nevertheless, the Umayyads still considered the complete subjugation of Byzantium as their ultimate objective. Their thinking was dominated by Islamic teaching, which placed the infidel Byzantines in the Dār al-Ḥarb, the "House of War." Rather than peace being interrupted by occasional conflict, the normal pattern was seen to be conflict interrupted by an occasional temporary truce. True peace could only come when the enemy accepted Islam or tributary status."

Both as governor of Syria and later as caliph, Muawiyah I (r. 661–680 A.D.)

was the driving force of the Muslim effort against Byzantium, especially by his creation of a fleet, which challenged the Byzantine navy and raided the Byzantine islands and coasts. To stop the Byzantine harassment from the sea during the Arab-Byzantine Wars, in 649 A.D. Muawiyah set up a navy, manned by Monophysitise Christians,

Copt, and Jacobite Syrian Christian sailors and Muslim troops. This resulted in the defeat of the Byzantine navy at the Battle of the Masts in 655 A.D., opening up the Mediterranean. The shocking defeat of the imperial fleet by the young Muslim navy at the Battle of the Masts in 655 A.D. was of critical importance: it opened up the Mediterranean, previously a "Roman lake", to Arab expansion, and began a centuries-long series of naval conflicts over the control of the Mediterranean waterways. 500 Byzantine ships were destroyed in the battle, and Emperor Constans II was almost killed. Under the instructions of the caliph Uthman ibn Affan, Muawiyah then prepared for the siege of Constantinople.

Muawiyah launched a series of attacks against Byzantine holdings in Africa, Sicily and the East. By 670 A.D., the Muslim fleet had penetrated into the Sea of Marmara and stayed at Cyzicus during the winter. Four years later, a massive Muslim fleet reappeared in the Marmara and re-established a base at Cyzicus, from there they raided the Byzantine coasts almost at will. Finally in 676 A.D., Muawiyah sent an army to invest Constantinople from land as well, beginning the First Arab Siege of the city. Constantine IV (r. 661–685 A.D.) however used a devastating new weapon that came to be known as "Greek fire" (an incendiary chemical weapon), invented by a Christian refugee from Syria named Kallinikos of Heliopolis, to decisively defeat the attacking Umayyad navy in the Sea of Marmara, resulting in the lifting of the siege in 678 A.D. The returning Muslim fleet suffered further losses due to storms, while the army lost many men to the armies who attacked them on their route back. Among those killed in the siege was Eyup, the standard bearer of Muhammed and the last of his companions. To Muslims today, his tomb is considered one of the holiest sites in Istanbul.

The setback at Constantinople was followed by further reverses across the vast Muslim empire. Then, the third governor of Africa, Zuheir, was overthrown by a powerful army, sent from Constantinople by Constantine IV for the relief of Carthage. Meanwhile, a second Arab civil war was raging in Arabia and Syria resulting in a series of four caliphs between the death of Muawiyah in 680 A.D. and the ascension of Abd al-Malik in 685 A.D., and was ongoing until 692 A.D. with the death of the rebel leader.

The Saracen Wars of Justinian II (685–695 A.D. and 705–711 A.D.), the last emperor of the Heraclian Dynasty, "reflected the general chaos of the age." After a successful campaign he made a truce with the Arabs, agreeing on joint possession of Armenia, Iberia and Cyprus; however, by removing 12,000 Christian Mardaites from their native Lebanon, he removed a major obstacle for the Arabs in Syria, and in 692 A.D., after the disastrous Battle of Sebastopolis, the Muslims invaded and conquered all of Armenia. Deposed in 695 A.D., with Carthage lost in 698 A.D., Justinian returned to power from 705 to 711 A.D. His second reign was marked by Arab victories in Asia Minor and civil unrest. Reportedly, he ordered his guards to execute the only unit that had not deserted him after one battle, to prevent their desertion in the next.

Justinian's first and second reigns were followed by internal disorder, with successive revolts and emperors lacking legitimacy or support. In this climate, the Umayyads consolidated their control of Armenia and Cilicia, and began preparing a renewed offensive against Constantinople. In Byzantium, the general Leo the Isaurian (717–741 A.D.) had just seized the throne in March 717 A.D., when the massive Muslim army under the famed Umayyad prince and general Maslama ibn Abd al-Malik began moving towards the imperial capital. The Caliphate's army and navy, led by Maslama, numbered some 120,000 men and 1,800 ships according to the sources. Whatever the real number, it was a huge force, far larger than the imperial army. Thankfully for Leo and the Empire, the capital's sea walls had recently been repaired and strengthened. In addition, the emperor concluded an alliance with the Bulgar khan Tervel, who agreed to harass the invaders' rear.

From July 717 A.D. to August 718 A.D., the city was besieged by land and sea by the Muslims isolating the capital. Their attempt to complete the blockade by sea however failed when the navy employed Greek fire against them; the Arab fleet kept well off the city walls, leaving Constantinople's supply routes open. Forced to extend the siege into winter, the besieging army suffered horrendous casualties from the cold and the lack of provisions.

In spring, new reinforcements were sent by the new caliph, Umar ibn Abd al-Aziz (717–720 A.D.), by sea from Africa and Egypt and over land through Asia Minor. The crews of the new fleets were composed mostly of Christians, who began defecting in large numbers, while the land forces were ambushed and defeated in Bithynia. As famine and an epidemic continued to plague the Arab camp, the siege was abandoned on August 718 A.D. On its return, the Arab fleet suffered further casualties to storms and an eruption of the volcano of Thera.

The first wave of the Muslim conquests ended with the siege of Constantinople in 718 A.D., and the border between the two empires became stabilized along the mountains of eastern Anatolia. Raids and counter-raids continued on both sides and became almost ritualized, but the prospect of outright conquest of Byzantium by the Caliphate receded. This led to far more regular, and often friendly, diplomatic contacts, as well as a reciprocal recognition of the two empires.

In response to the Muslim threat, which reached its peak in the first half of the 8th century, the Isaurian emperors adopted the policy of Iconoclasm, which was abandoned in 786 A.D. only to be readopted in the 820s A.D. and finally abandoned in 843 A.D. Under the Macedonian dynasty, exploiting the decline and fragmentation of the Abbasid Caliphate, the Byzantines gradually went on the offensive, and recovered much territory in the 10th century.

The Third Council of Constantinople – 680 to 681 A.D.

The Third Council of Constantinople, also known as the Sixth Ecumenical Council, convened in 680–681 A.D. It was summoned by Emperor Constantine IV and held in Constantinople. The council addressed the Monothelitism controversy, which centered around the question of whether Christ had one will or two.

Here are the key points about the Third Council of Constantinople:

1. Background:

   a. The theological controversies leading up to this council dated back to the sixth century but had intensified under the emperors Heraclius and Constans II.

   b. Heraclius attempted to reconcile the controversy with monophysitism (strongly present in Syria and Egypt) by proposing a moderate theological position.

   c. This resulted in two related doctrines: monoenergism (asserting that Christ had one energy despite existing in two natures) and monothelitism (claiming that Christ had only one will, without opposition between his human and divine volition).

2. Council Decisions:

   a. The Third Council of Constantinople condemned both Monoenergism and monothelitism as heretical.

   b. It defined that Jesus Christ possessed two energies (divine and human) and two wills (divine and human).

3. Significance:

   a. he council's decisions clarified the nature of Christ's will and energy, emphasizing the duality of his divine and human aspects.

   b. It reaffirmed the orthodox position against monothelitism and monoenergism.

In summary, the Third Council of Constantinople played a crucial role in resolving theological disputes related to Christ's nature and will, contributing to the development of Christian doctrine.

In 732 A.D. another conflict ensued in The Battle of Tours, also called the Battle of Poitiers and the Battle of the Highway of the Martyrs. This was an important battle during the Umayyad invasion of Gaul (France). It resulted in victory for the Frankish and Aquitanian forces, led by Charles Martel, over the invading Muslim forces of the Umayyad Caliphate, led by Abd al-Rahman al-Ghafiqi, governor of al-Andalus. Several historians have credited the Christian victory in the battle as an important factor in curtailing the Islamization of Western Europe.

Most sources agree that the Umayyads had a larger force and suffered heavier casualties. Notably, the Frankish troops apparently fought without heavy cavalry. The battlefield was located somewhere between the cities of Poitiers and Tours, in northern Aquitaine in western France, near the border of the Frankish realm and the then-independent Duchy of Aquitaine under Odo the Great.

Al-Ghafiqi was killed in combat, and the Umayyad army withdrew after the battle. The battle helped lay the foundations of the Carolingian Empire and Frankish domination of western Europe for the next century. Most historians agree that "the establishment of Frankish power in western Europe shaped that continent's destiny and the Battle of Tours confirmed that power."

The Second Council of Nicaea – 787 A.D.

The Second Council of Nicaea is recognized as the last of the first seven ecumenical councils by the Eastern Orthodox church and the Catholic church. In addition, it is also recognized as such by the Old Catholics, and others.

The council met in 787 A.D. in Nicaea (site of the First Council of Nicaea; present-day İznik, Bursa, in Turkey), to restore the use and veneration of icons (or holy images), which had been suppressed by imperial edict inside the Byzantine Empire during the reign of Leo III (717–741 A.D.). His son Constantine V (741–775 A.D.), had held the Council of Hieria to make the suppression official.

There was debate over whether bishops who had accepted iconoclasm when under iconoclast rule could remain in office. Letters from Pope Adrian I were read out in Greek translation, approving the reverence of images, but severely critical of Byzantine infringement of papal rights. Accepting the letter at the papal representative's prompting, the bishops answered: "We follow, we receive, we admit."

The supposed representatives of the oriental patriarchates presented their credentials. From these it is clear that their patriarchs had not in fact appointed them.

Proof of the lawfulness of the reverence of icons was drawn from Exodus 25:19; Numbers 7:89; Hebrews 9:5.; Ezekiel 41:18, and Genesis 31:34, but especially from a series of passages of the church Fathers; and from hagiography.

A further statement was read out, "proving" that iconoclasm originated from pagans, Jews, Muslims, and heretics. The definition of the pseudo-Seventh council (754 A.D.) and a long rejection of the same (probably by Tarasius) were read. The council issued a declaration of faith concerning the reverence of holy images. It was determined that:

As the sacred and life-giving cross is everywhere set up as a symbol, so also should the images of Jesus Christ, the Virgin Mary, the holy angels, as well as those of the saints and other pious and holy men be embodied in the manufacture of sacred vessels, tapestries, vestments, etc., and exhibited on the walls of churches, in the homes, and in all conspicuous places, by the roadside and everywhere, to be revered by all who might see them. For the more they are contemplated, the more they move to fervent memory of their prototypes. Therefore, it is proper to accord to them a fervent and reverent veneration, not, however, the veritable adoration which, according to our faith, belongs to the Divine Being alone—for the honor accorded to the image passes over to its prototype, and whoever venerate the image venerate in it the reality of what is there represented.

The twenty-two canons drawn up in Constantinople also served ecclesiastical reform. Careful maintenance of the ordinances of the earlier councils, knowledge of the scriptures on the part of the clergy, and care for Christian conduct are required, and the desire for a renewal of ecclesiastical life is awakened.

The council also decreed that every altar should contain a relic, which remains the case in modern Catholic and Orthodox regulations (Canon VII), and made a number of decrees on clerical discipline, especially for monks when mixing with women.

It is particularly interesting that four Dalmatian bishops are among the signatories of the synod, whose cities were no longer under Byzantine rule. These Dalmatian dioceses had been dissolved earlier. So, the question arises when were these dioceses re-established in these medieval Dalmatian cities?

This suggests that new diocese was founded or old (Early Christian) episcopal seats were re-established in this area. The founding of these diocese is attested by the 8th century Chronicon Gradense. The chronicle reports the foundation of several Dalmatian diocese, such as the diocese of Rab as "Avoriciensis/ Avonciensis ecclesia", the foundation of the diocese of Krk as "episcopatus in Vegla", the foundation of the diocese of Osor as "episcopatus in Asparo", and the diocese of Pićan as "episcopus Pathensis." As the chronicle reports a Dalmatian provincial synod held in the city of Grado.

Later in 800 A.D. Charlemagne was crowned the emperor of the Holy Roman Empire by Pope Leo III and Christian missionaries developed the Cyrillic alphabet in 858 A.D; used in 50+ languages today including Russian, Serbian, Bulgarian, and Belarusian. Prince Boris of Bulgaria was baptized, leading to the establishment of the Bulgarian church in 864 A.D. Rollo and his Vikings converted to Christianity in 912 A.D. And Prince Vladimir was baptized, which begins the conversion of the Russian people to Christianity in 988 A.D.

THE GREAT EAST-WEST SCHISM – 1054 A.D.

Tensions continued to grow in the church and were now reaching the boiling point. As tensions mounted between the Eastern church in Constantinople and the Western church in Rome, the breaking point was at hand. The churches in the East were developing distinct cultural and theological differences from those in the West. Tensions gradually increased between the two branches, and finally reached its climax in 1054 A.D. with the Great East-West Schism.

East and West tensions had been escalating going as far back as the fourth century. The Great Schism of 1054 A.D. marked the first major split in the history of Christianity, separating the Orthodox church in the East from the Roman Catholic church in the West.

By the third century, the Roman Empire was growing too large and difficult to govern, so Emperor Diocletian decided to divide the empire into two domains —the Western Roman Empire and the Eastern Roman Empire, also known as the Byzantine Empire. One of the initial factors which caused a shifting apart of the two domains was language. The primary language in the West was Latin, while the dominant language in the East was Greek. Eastern churches developed Greek rites, using the Greek language in their religious ceremonies and the Greek Septuagint translation of the Old Testament. Roman churches conducted services in Latin, and their Bibles were written in the Latin Vulgate.

During this time, several groups who disagreed with aspects of doctrine codified during one or more of the seven ecumenical councils broke away from the church and followed their own teachings. This patchwork of offshoots from the Roman Catholic church are known as pre-schism churches. These include the Coptic Christians in Egypt, the Armenian Apostolic church, Coptic Orthodox church of Alexandria, Ethiopian Orthodox Tewahedo church, Eritrean Orthodox Tewahedo church, Malankara Orthodox Syrian church, the Syriac Orthodox church of Antioch, and some others.

There were many factors in this split. It is important to consider here the rise of Islam in the Middle East, which from the 7th century began conquering Christian territory and reducing the influence of the Roman Empire.

At the heart of the break was the Roman pope's claim to universal jurisdiction and authority. The Orthodox church in the East had agreed to honor the pope but believed that ecclesiastical matters should be decided by a council of bishops, and therefore, would not grant unchallenged dominion to the pope.

The churches in the divided Empire began to disconnect as well. Five patriarchs held authority in different regions: The Patriarch of Rome,

Alexandria, Antioch, Constantinople, and Jerusalem. The Patriarch of Rome (the pope) held the honor of "first among equals," but he did not possess authority over the other patriarchs. Small disagreements called "little schisms" took place in the centuries leading up to the Great Schism. The first little schism (343-398 A.D.) was over Arianism, a belief that denied Jesus to be of the same substance as God or equal to God, and therefore not divine. This belief was accepted by many in the Eastern church but rejected by the Western church.

Another little schism, the Acacian Schism (482-519 A.D.), had to do with an argument over the nature of the incarnate Christ, specifically whether Jesus Christ had one divine-human nature or two distinct natures (divine and human). One other little schism, known as the Photian Schism, occurred during the ninth century. The dividing issues centered on clerical celibacy, fasting, anointing with oil, and the procession of the Holy Spirit.

Although temporary, these splits between East and West led to embittered relations as the two branches of Christianity grew further and further apart. Theologically, the East and West had taken separate paths. The Latin approach generally leaned to the practical, while the Greek mindset was more mystical and speculative. Latin thought was strongly influenced by Roman law and scholastic theology, while Greeks comprehended theology through philosophy and the context of worship.

Practical and spiritual differences existed between the two branches. For instance, the churches disagreed on whether it was acceptable to use unleavened bread for communion ceremonies. Western churches supported the practice, while Greeks used leavened bread in the Eucharist. Eastern churches allowed their priests to marry, while Latins insisted on celibacy.

Eventually, the influence of the patriarchs of Antioch, Jerusalem, and Alexandria began to weaken, bringing Rome and Constantinople to the forefront as the two power centers of the church.

During the eighth and ninth centuries, controversy also arose regarding the use of icons in worship. Byzantine Emperor Leo III declared that the worship of religious images was heretical and idolatrous. Many Eastern bishops cooperated with their emperor's rule, but the Western Church stood firm in support of the use of religious images. https://www.learnreligions.com/the-great-schism-of-1054-4691893

The filioque clause (a phrase added to the Nicene Creed in the Western Church) controversy ignited one of the most critical arguments of the East-West Schism. This dispute centered around the Trinity doctrine and whether the Holy Spirit proceeds from God the Father alone or from both the Father and the Son.

Filioque is a Latin term meaning "and the son." Originally, the Nicene

Creed stated simply that the Holy Spirit "proceeds from the Father," a phrase intended to defend the divinity of the Holy Spirit. The filioque clause was added to the creed by the Western church to suggest that the Holy Spirit proceeds from both the Father "and the Son."

The Eastern church insisted on keeping the original wording of the Nicene Creed, leaving the filioque clause out. Leaders in the East argued loudly that the West had no right to alter the foundational creed of Christianity without consulting the Eastern church. Furthermore, they felt the addition revealed underlying theological differences between the two branches and their understanding of the Trinity. The Eastern church thought itself to be the only true and right one, believing Western theology to be based erroneously in Augustinian thinking, which they considered heterodox, which means unorthodox and verging on heretical.

Leaders on both sides refused to budge on the filioque issue. Eastern bishops began accusing the pope and bishops in the West of heresy. In the end, the two churches forbade the use of the other church's rites and excommunicated one another from the true Christian church.

Most contentious of all and the conflict which brought the Great Schism to a head was the issue of ecclesiastical authority—specifically, whether the pope in Rome held power over the patriarchs in the East. The Roman church had argued for the primacy of the Roman pope since the fourth century and claimed that he held universal authority over the whole church. Eastern leaders honored the pope but refused to grant him the power to determine policy for other jurisdictions or to alter the decisions of Ecumenical Councils.

In the years leading up to the Great Schism, the church in the East was led by the Patriarch of Constantinople, Michael Cerularius (1000–1058 A.D.), while the church in Rome was led by Pope Leo IX (1002–1054 A.D.).

At the time, problems sprang up in Southern Italy, which was part of the Byzantine Empire. Norman warriors had invaded, conquering the region and replacing Greek bishops with Latin ones. When Cerularius learned that the Normans were forbidding Greek rites in the churches of Southern Italy, he retaliated by shutting down the Latin rite churches in Constantinople.

Their longstanding disputes erupted when Pope Leo sent his chief advisor Cardinal Humbert to Constantinople with instructions to deal with the problem. Humbert aggressively criticized and condemned the actions of Cerularius.

When Cerularius ignored the pope's demands, he was formally excommunicated as Patriarch of Constantinople on July 16, 1054 A.D. In response, Cerularius burned the papal decree of excommunication and declared the bishop of Rome to be a heretic. The East-West Schism was sealed.

Even after the great split, attempts were made at reconciliation. The two branches still communicated with each other on friendly terms until the time of the Fourth Crusade. However, in 1204 A.D., Western crusaders brutally sacked Constantinople and defiled the great Byzantine church of the Hagia Sophia. An attempt at reconciliation took place at the Second Council of Lyon in 1274 A.D., but the accord was flatly rejected by the bishops of the East. Now that the break was permanent, the two branches of Christianity became more and more divided doctrinally, politically, and on liturgical matters.

The Crusades to the East were in every way defensive wars. They were a direct response to Muslim aggression—an attempt to turn back or defend against Muslim conquests of Christian lands.

Christians in the eleventh century were not paranoid fanatics. Muslims really were gunning for them. While Muslims can be peaceful, Islam was born in war and grew the same way. From the time of Mohammed, the means of Muslim expansion was always the sword.

Muslim thought divides the world into two spheres, the abode of Islam and the abode of War. Christianity—and for that matter any other non-Muslim religion—has no abode. Christians and Jews can be tolerated within a Muslim state under Muslim rule. But, in traditional Islam, Christian and Jewish states must be destroyed and their lands conquered. When Mohammed was waging war against Mecca in the seventh century, Christianity was the dominant religion of power and wealth. As the faith of the Roman Empire, it spanned the entire Mediterranean, including the Middle East, where it was born. The Christian world, therefore, was a prime target for the earliest caliphs, and it would remain so for Muslim leaders for the next thousand years.

The Byzantine Empire, was reduced to little more than Greece. In desperation, the emperor in Constantinople sent word to the Christians of Western Europe asking them to aid their brothers and sisters in the East.

That is what gave birth to the Crusades. They were not the brainchild of an ambitious pope or rapacious knights but a response to more than four centuries of conquests in which Muslims had already captured two-thirds of the old Christian world. At some point, Christianity as a faith and a culture had to defend itself or be subsumed by Islam. The Crusades were that defense.

COUNCIL OF CLERMONT 1095 A.D.

An assembly for church reform called by Pope Urban II on November 18, 1095 A.D., which became the occasion for initiating the First Crusade. The Council was attended largely by bishops of southern France as well as a few representatives from northern France and elsewhere. As a result of a request by envoys from the Byzantine emperor Alexius I Comnenus to aid the Greeks against the Muslim Turks, Urban II exhorted the French knights at Clermont to rescue the Holy Land from the Turks. Much important ecclesiastical business was transacted, which resulted in a series of canons, among them one that renewed the Peace of God and another that granted a remission of all penance for sin to those who undertook to aid Christians in the East. Then, in a great outdoor assembly, the Pope, a Frenchman, addressed a large crowd, closing his speech with the words "God wills it," which became a battle cry of the Crusaders.

The response was tremendous. Many thousands of warriors took the vow of the cross and prepared for war. Why did they do it? The answer to that question has been badly misunderstood. In the wake of the Enlightenment, it was usually asserted that Crusaders were merely lacklands and slackers who took advantage of an opportunity to rob and pillage in a faraway land. The Crusaders' expressed sentiments of piety, self-sacrifice, and love for God were obviously not to be taken seriously. They were only a front for darker designs.

The Crusaders willingly gave up everything to undertake the holy mission. Crusading was not cheap. Even wealthy lords could easily impoverish themselves and their families by joining a Crusade. They did so not because they expected material wealth (which many of them had already) but because they hoped to store up treasure where rust and moth could not corrupt. They were keenly aware of their sinfulness and eager to undertake the hardships of the Crusade as an act of charity and love. Europe is littered with thousands of medieval charters attesting to these sentiments, charters in which these men still speak to us today if we will listen. Of course, they were not opposed to capturing booty if it could be had. But the truth is that the Crusades were notoriously bad for plunder. A few people got rich, but the vast majority returned with nothing.

The Crusaders had two goals: The first was to rescue the Christians of the East. The Crusades were seen as an errand of mercy to right a terrible wrong. As Pope Innocent III wrote to the Knights Templar, "You carry out in deeds the words of the Gospel, 'Greater love than this hath no man, that he lay down his life for his friends.'"

The second goal was the liberation of Jerusalem and the other places made holy by the life of Christ. Medieval Crusaders saw themselves as pilgrims, performing acts of righteousness on their way to the Holy Sepulcher.

By any reckoning, the First Crusade was a long shot. There was no leader, no chain of command, no supply lines, no detailed strategy. It was simply thousands of warriors marching deep into enemy territory, committed to a common cause. Many of them died, either in battle or through disease or starvation. It was a rough campaign, one that seemed always on the brink of disaster. Yet it was miraculously successful. By 1098 A.D., the Crusaders had restored Nicaea and Antioch to Christian rule. In July 1099 A.D., they conquered Jerusalem and began to build a Christian state in Palestine. The joy in Europe was unbridled. It seemed that the tide of history, which had lifted the Muslims to such heights, was now turning.

Or was it! When we think about the Middle Ages, it is easy to view Europe in light of what it became rather than what it was. The colossus of the medieval world was Islam, not Christendom. The Crusades are interesting largely because they were an attempt to counter that trend. But in five centuries of crusading, it was only the First Crusade that significantly rolled back the military progress of Islam. It was downhill from there.

When Edessa fell to the Turks and Kurds in 1144 A.D., there was an enormous groundswell of support for a new Crusade in Europe. It was led by two kings, Louis VII of France and Conrad III of Germany, and preached by St. Bernard himself. It failed miserably. Most of the Crusaders were killed along the way. Those who made it to Jerusalem only made things worse by attacking Muslim Damascus, which formerly had been a strong ally of the Christians. In the wake of such a disaster, Christians across Europe were forced to accept not only the continued growth of Muslim power but the certainty that God was punishing the West for its sins. Virtue movements sprouted up throughout Europe, all rooted in the desire to purify Christian society so that it might be worthy of victory in the East.

Crusading in the late twelfth century, therefore, became a total war effort. Every person, no matter how weak or poor, was called to help. Warriors were asked to sacrifice their wealth and, if need be, their lives for the defense of the Christian East. On the home front, all Christians were called to support the Crusades through prayer, fasting, and alms. Yet still the Muslims grew in strength. Saladin, the great unifier, had forged the Muslim Near East into a single entity, all the while preaching jihad against the Christians. In 1187 A.D. at the Battle of Hattin, his forces wiped out the combined armies of the Christian Kingdom of Jerusalem and captured the precious relic of the True Cross. Defenseless, the Christian cities began surrendering one by one, culminating in the surrender of Jerusalem on October 2. Only a tiny handful of ports held out.

The response was the Third Crusade. It was led by Emperor Frederick I Barbarossa of the German Empire, King Philip II Augustus of France, and King Richard I Lionheart of England. By any measure it was a grand affair, although not quite as grand as the Christians had hoped. The aged Frederick drowned while crossing a river on horseback, so his army returned home before reaching the Holy Land. Philip and Richard came by boat, but their incessant bickering only added to an already divisive situation on the ground in Palestine. After recapturing Acre, the king of France went home, where he busied himself carving up Richard's French holdings. The Crusade, therefore, fell into Richard's lap. A skilled warrior, gifted leader, and superb tactician, Richard led the Christian forces to victory after victory, eventually reconquering the entire coast. But Jerusalem was not on the coast, and after two abortive attempts to secure supply lines to the Holy City, Richard at last gave up. Promising to return one day, he struck a truce with Saladin that ensured peace in the region and free access to Jerusalem for unarmed pilgrims. But it was a bitter pill to swallow. The desire to restore Jerusalem to Christian rule and regain the True Cross remained intense throughout Europe.

The Crusades of the 13th century were larger, better funded, and better organized. But they too failed. The Fourth Crusade (1201-1204 A.D.) ran aground when it was seduced into a web of Byzantine politics, which the Westerners never fully understood. They had made a detour to Constantinople to support an imperial claimant who promised great rewards and support for the Holy Land. Yet once he was on the throne of the Caesars, their benefactor found that he could not pay what he had promised. Thus, betrayed by their Greek friends, in 1204 A.D. the Crusaders attacked, captured, and brutally sacked Constantinople, the greatest Christian city in the world. Pope Innocent III, who had previously excommunicated the entire Crusade, strongly denounced the Crusaders. But there was little else he could do. The tragic events of 1204 A.D. closed an iron door between Roman Catholic and Greek Orthodox. It is a terrible irony that the Crusades, which were a direct result of the Catholic desire to rescue the Orthodox people, drove the two further—and perhaps irrevocably—apart.

The remainder of the 13th century's Crusades did little better. The Fifth Crusade (1217-1221 A.D.) managed briefly to capture Damietta in Egypt, but the Muslims eventually defeated the army and reoccupied the city. St. Louis IX of France led two Crusades in his life. The first also captured Damietta, but Louis was quickly outwitted by the Egyptians and forced to abandon the city. Although Louis was in the Holy Land for several years, spending freely on defensive works, he never achieved his fondest wish: to free Jerusalem. He was a much older man in 1270 A.D. when he led another Crusade to Tunis, where he died of a disease that ravaged the camp. After St. Louis's death, the ruthless Muslim leaders, Baybars and Kalavun, waged a brutal jihad against the Christians in Palestine. By 1291 A.D., the Muslim forces had succeeded in killing or ejecting the last of the Crusaders, thus erasing the Crusader kingdom from the map. Despite numerous attempts and many more plans, Christian forces were never again able to gain a foothold in the region until the

19th century.

One might think that three centuries of Christian defeats would have soured Europeans on the idea of a Crusade. Not at all. In one sense, they had little alternative. Muslim kingdoms were becoming more, not less, powerful in the 14th, 15th, and 16th centuries. The Ottoman Turks conquered not only their fellow Muslims, thus further unifying Islam, but also continued to press westward, capturing Constantinople and plunging deep into Europe itself. By the 15th century, the Crusades were no longer errands of mercy for a distant people but desperate attempts of one of the last remnants of Christendom to survive. Europeans began to ponder the real possibility that Islam would finally achieve its aim of conquering the entire Christian world. One voice to this sentiment follows:

Our faith was strong in th' Orient, it ruled in all of Asia, In Moorish lands and Africa. But now for us these lands are gone 'Twould even grieve the hardest stone.... Four sisters of our Church you find, They're of the patriarchic kind: Constantinople, Alexandria, Jerusalem, Antiochia. But they've been forfeited and sacked and soon the head will be attacked.

Of course, that is not what happened. But it very nearly did. In 1480 A.D., Sultan Mehmed II captured Otranto as a beachhead for his invasion of Italy. Rome was evacuated. Yet the sultan died shortly thereafter, and his plan died with him. In 1529 A.D., Suleiman the Magnificent laid siege to Vienna. If not for a run of freak rainstorms that delayed his progress and forced him to leave behind much of his artillery, it is virtually certain that the Turks would have taken the city. Germany, then, would have been at their mercy.

Yet, even while these close shaves were taking place, something else was brewing in Europe—something unprecedented in human history. The Renaissance, born from a strange mixture of Roman values, medieval piety, and a unique respect for commerce and entrepreneurialism, had led to other movements like humanism, the Scientific Revolution, and the Age of Exploration. Even while fighting for its life, Europe was preparing to expand on a global scale.

In 1571 A.D., a Holy League, which was itself a Crusade, defeated the Ottoman fleet at Lepanto. Yet military victories like that remained rare. The Muslim threat was neutralized economically. As Europe grew in wealth and power, the once awesome and sophisticated Turks began to seem backward and pathetic —no longer worth a Crusade. The "Sick Man of Europe" limped along until the 20th century, when he finally expired, leaving behind the present mess of the modern Middle East.

From the safe distance of many centuries, it is easy enough to scowl in disgust at the Crusades. Religion, after all, is nothing to fight wars over. But we should be mindful that our medieval ancestors would have been equally disgusted by our infinitely more destructive wars fought in the name of political ideologies.

And yet, both the medieval and the modern soldier fight ultimately for their own world and all that makes it up. Both are willing to suffer enormous sacrifice, provided that it is in the service of something they hold dear, something greater than themselves. Whether we admire the Crusaders or not, it is a fact that the world we know today would not exist without their efforts. The ancient faith of Christianity, with its respect for women and antipathy toward slavery, not only survived but flourished. Without the Crusades, it might well have followed Zoroastrianism, another of Islam's rivals, into extinction. https://crisismagazine.com/opinion/the-real-history-of-the-crusades. https://www.britannica.com/event/Council-of-Clermont.

THE PROTESTANT REFORMATION
1517 A.D. – PRESENT DAY

So, if we go back to the year 1500 A.D., the church (what we now call the Roman Catholic church) was very powerful (politically and spiritually) in Western Europe (and in fact ruled over significant territory in Italy called the Papal States). But there were other political forces at work too. There was the Holy Roman Empire (largely made up of German speaking regions ruled by princes, dukes, and electors), the Italian city-states, England, as well as the increasingly unified nation states of France and Spain among others.

Keep in mind too, that for some time the church had been seen as an institution plagued by internal power struggles (at one point in the late 1300s and 1400s A.D. church was ruled by three Popes simultaneously). Popes and cardinals often lived more like kings than spiritual leaders. Popes claimed temporal (political) as well as spiritual power. They commanded armies, made political alliances and enemies, and, sometimes, even waged war. Simony (the selling of church offices) and nepotism (favoritism based on family relationships) were rampant. Clearly, if the Pope was concentrating on these worldly issues, there wasn't as much time left for caring for the souls of the faithful. The corruption of the church was well known, and several attempts had been made to reform the church, but none of these efforts successfully challenged church practice until Martin Luther's actions in the early 1500s. https://www.khanacademy.org/humanities/renaissance-reformation/reformation-counterreformation/beginner-guide-reforrmation/a/the-protestant-reformation.

John Wycliffe (1330-1384 A.D.) is credited with being one of the first reformers. Although he never led The Reformation, he was an influential critic of the Catholic church. Wycliffe took a very strong stance on the authority of the Bible right along the vein of what would eventually become the Protestant Reformation. His works were well known, and highly influential, among the reformers and also a Bohemian bishop named Jan Hus. Wycliffe is credited with producing one of the first English translations of the Bible, designed for mass consumption.

Jan Hus, in the early 15th century in Moravia (modern day Czech Republic), picked up Wycliffe's teachings and spread them throughout Bohemia and Moravia where they became wildly popular. His followers became the Hussites. Shortly prior to The Reformation, several wars almost extinguished the Hussites. However, a very small number survived. When The Reformation arrived, most of these forerunners assimilated with the new reformers.

On October 31, 1517 Martin Luther strolled up to the All-Saint's church in Wittenberg, and slammed his 95 theses on the front door. This article stipulated, in Luther's view, the serious errors that the Catholic church needed to address. Most important of these was his firm conviction that by God's grace alone, are we able to be saved from God's judgement. That and the Bible (not the Pope, or tradition) was the sole authority on matters of faith and teaching. In short, the Bible was God's inspired Word, and the Pope was just another sinner, just like the rest of us.

According to Luther, the Popes word was not infallible, and he had *no* power to forgive sins. Luther was not the first to take issue with the church, but he struck a chord.

Thanks in large part to the printing press (one of the many technological advancements achieved during the Middle Ages), Luther's 95 thesis went viral, and sparked a firestorm of controversy.

In 1520 A.D. Martin Luther was branded a heretic so he shook his sandals of the Catholic church and started a revolution... or a 'Reformation' if you will. By the time he got back to Wittenberg, Luther's influence had exploded and had taken on a life of its own.

At around-about the same time, in Zurich, another zealous preacher by the name of Huldrich Zwingli was resisting the church in a very similar vein to Luther, gaining momentum in what would become the reformed tradition.

Another important consideration here was the rise of the Black Plague, which decimated London no less than 6 times from 1563 – 1667 A.D., almost perfectly coinciding with The Reformation. Every time there was an outbreak it took 10-30% of the population!!

Eventually, the reformers codified their beliefs into what is known as the five solas:

1. Sola scriptura – 'scripture alone'

2. Sola fide – 'faith alone'

3. Sola gratia – 'grace alone'

4. Solo Christo – 'Christ alone'

5. Soli Deo Gloria – 'to the glory of God alone'

Following Martin Luther, sects began popping up everywhere for all sorts of reasons. Most of these were reactions to Catholic practices and beliefs that they believed weren't in the Bible. The Catholic church went to great lengths to restore order, and quell the rise of these dissenters. In 1529 the Lutherans and other reformers were officially labeled 'protestants', a term they quickly embraced, and wore as a badge of honor.

Around the same time as the protestant Reformation, the Catholic church launched a 'counter-Reformation', and in 1545 A.D. held the Council of Trent, an ecumenical council, specifically to deal with the startling rise of protestant groups across the Western Empire.

Time went on, denominations continued to pop up all over the place, and internal disagreements and changes in focus continued to spawn Christian sects. Some denominations began to diverge simply due to geographical isolation. As time went by, some denominations began to see such diversity as a problem, and make an effort to reconcile and form larger communions.

Some came to see the idea of 'Christian denominations' as divisive and have sought to dispense with the term altogether. The landscape of Christianity has evolved over time, morphing into a complex array of denominations all with their own unique flavors.

As the centuries went by denominations and their differences changed. They were less about their gripes with the Catholic church and more about their responses to the ever evolving cultural, economic and moral landscape that surrounded them.

Many of the largest and oldest Christian denominations have split at some point into two major sub-denominations, often based on how conservatively the original group held to the truth of the Bible. This in turn affects how they view many modern social and political issues, which can lead to rather significant differences between them.

Finally, you have the individual believers, every one of whom is in some way unique. Everyone is a product of their own level of understanding of the Bible, and their own values and personal study (or lack of it). The Reformation would forever change the landscape of Western Civilization.

Movements, Not Denominations

Before we dive into different denominations, there are a number of well-known terms often used to describe certain groups of Christians, or movements, but are not specific denominations themselves. These movements include the following:

Calvinism

Calvinism is a branch of Christian Theology developed and popularized by John Calvin, summarized in what are described as the 'five points' of Calvinist theology (affectionately referred to as TULIP).

1. Total depravity

2. Unconditional election

3. Limited atonement

4. Irresistible Grace

5. Perseverance of the Saints

These five points are by no means all that Calvinists preach and believe, but are considered the defining characteristics. While not a denomination specifically, several denominations are rooted in reformed theology. In fact, many proponents prefer the term 'reformed' to 'Calvinist', because reformed theology did not originate with Calvin. There were others before him (like Huldrich Zwingli). Denominations with strong Calvinist roots are the Reformed, the Presbyterians and Reformed Baptists.

However, you can find examples of other denominations with major branches adopting either a more Arminian, or reformed theology such as the Brethren and some Baptist churches.

Arminianism

Arminianism is the antithesis of reformed theology. While Calvinism emphasizes the total sovereignty of God, Arminianism emphasizes mankind's free will to either choose, or reject God. The Arminian believes that while God is completely omnipotent, and has a perfect overarching plan for mankind, we are each individually free to choose to accept God's grace, or to reject it.

Like Calvinism, Arminianism is also not a denomination, but a branch of theology which runs deeply through a great many denominations and schools of Christian thought. Examples of strongly Arminian denominations include Baptists, Methodists, Pentecostals and many non-denominational churches, and more.

Molinism

If Calvinism emphasizes God's sovereignty and Arminianism emphasizes man's free will, then Molinism tries really hard to explain them both. Somewhat surprisingly, Molinism is a less widespread system of philosophical theology pioneered by 16th-century Jesuit, Luis de Molina, which advocates for a concept known as 'middle knowledge'.

Molinism tries to answer the question: 'How is it possible that God can know and be in control of everything, but we can still be held responsible for our actions?' It is a more sophisticated attempt to reconcile human free will, without limiting God's sovereignty and is advocated by some of the present day's most prolific Christian philosophers. Perhaps the two most well-known advocates of Molinism today are William Lane Craig, and Alvin Plantinga.

Evangelicals

If you spent a month researching the topic of 'evangelical Christian' and still weren't entirely, exactly sure what it meant, you wouldn't be alone. The term 'evangelical' is taken from the Greek 'Evangelion', and is just a fancy word for 'Gospel', which is just a fancy word to describe the core message of Christianity (the Good News that our sins can be forgiven through Jesus Christ). So evangelical Christians are, Christians, basically. The simplest understanding of the term is essentially any Christian who takes a strong stance on the authority of the Bible, who cares about evangelism (obviously), and generally adheres to the fundamentals of the Christian faith. If the term 'evangelical' has any real meaning, it is as somewhat of a contrast to the 'mainline' denominations.

They are perhaps the major sub-branches of mainline denominations which split away at some point, because they believed the mainline denominations were pushing too much away from the Bible's clear teachings, and more toward theological, social and moral liberalism (again, HUGE generalization!).

Fundamentalism

Technically, Christian fundamentalism is just a term that describes those Christians who adhere to the fundamentals of the Christian faith. In the modern sense however, the word refers to a particular movement.

Around the turn of the 20th Century, there was concern that the 'mainline' denominations were shifting away from a traditional, biblical commitment to Christian doctrine. Most significantly by undermining the authority of the Bible as God's inerrant Word. Basically, these guys were worried that Christians were starting to lose the faith, but not the title of 'Christian'.

Thus, a significant work was commissioned by a number of prominent conservative Christians, including John Nelson Darby, and Dwight L. Moody. The result was a large collection of writings available today as a two-volume set outlining the 'fundamentals of the Christian Faith'. In short, there are six main points:

1. The Bible is true, and error free

2. Mary was a virgin when she conceived Christ (which means it was a miracle)

3. Jesus Christ is fully God (the focal definition of Christianity)

4. Salvation is by grace alone (God's undeserved forgiveness), through faith alone (genuine belief in Christ's death and resurrection on the Cross)

5. When Christ rose from the dead, he did so in full human bodily form (he could eat food, be touched, etc.)

6. That Jesus will truly, and physically return to earth in what's known as the 'second coming'

Today the term is often used derisively, and has developed a negative connotation, which is a shame.

Ultimately, a 'fundamental' Christian, is just a Christian who believes the Bible is God's Word, and attempts to live their life in light of the Bibles message, understanding it as it was plainly intended to be understood.

Orthodox

The term Orthodox by itself simply refers to any set of beliefs which are considered the most 'original' or 'accepted' beliefs. For Christians it refers more specifically to Christians who most closely represent the original 'creeds' of Christianity, including especially the Nicene Creed and the Apostles Creed. The term also refers to 'Eastern Orthodox' Christians, which is a specific and major branch of Christianity.

The Roman church had long been held in special honor because Rome was the capital city of the Empire (before Constantinople). It was also the largest church by far with over 30,000 members by the Fourth Century, and because it was founded by Peter and Paul.

The term Pope was more or less used to refer to any bishop prior to the fourth century. In the fifth century, Pope Leo I is credited with one of the first claims to absolute papal authority. Leo laid out the biblical foundations for the papacy, and for the primacy of the Pope, as the rightful successor to St Peter, and head of the whole church.

Pope Leo I was also an ardent opponent of rising heresies, and a powerful ambassador for the Roman people. He spoke face to face with Attila the Hun and was the one who persuaded him not to sack Rome. He was also then responsible for staying the hand of the Vandals who, instead of burning Rome to the ground, plundered it and left the city unscathed, and with virtually no bloodshed.

In 590 A.D., Pope Gregory I officially instituted the Papal States, by consolidating the churches power over all lands controlled by the Pope. As the church evolved and its power expanded, so did its teachings, its hierarchy and its influence.

The Roman church developed into a highly complex theological and political system beginning at the Pope as the supreme leader of the church, with a cascading system of leadership all the way down to the local parish. The church became an extremely powerful force throughout the Middle Ages.

Very early on during The Reformation, the Catholic church held the council of Trent over a series of 25 sessions, spanning almost 20 years (1545-1563 A.D.), in order to deal specifically with the circumstances of The Reformation. The council of Trent, the 19th ecumenical council and the last council for the next 300 years, firmly established an everlasting split between the protestants, and the Catholic church.

As mentioned, Catholics themselves believe their history can be traced back to Peter, the original leader of the church. Virtually all other Christian denominations that exist today are the result of a split from the Catholic tradition, or of some internal split within some denomination which at some point or another split from the Catholic tradition.

The Roman Catholic church was the dominant religion throughout the Middle Ages (despite the rise of Islam) and has remained this way for almost its entire history, and therefore has had enormous influence over the development of the entire Western World. Source: A History of the Early church, (05 BC-AD 451), John A. Apeabu (Ph.D.). Department of Christian Religious Studies, Federal College of Education, Zaria. Ii, © 2020 John A. Apeabu (Ph. D)

Christian Denominations

Lutherans

"For no prophecy was ever produced by the will of man, but men spoke from God as they were carried along by the Holy Spirit." 2 Peter 1:21

The Lutheran church is in some respects, the godfather of all of modern Protestantism. It is *the* denomination which directly traces its ancestry back to Martin Luther, from whom, almost all of modern protestant denominations can trace their history to and it is the one which bears his name.

Luther in many ways was the most conservative of the reformers. He had specific issues that he wanted the church to address, but otherwise he saw no reason to radically alter the church. As a result, Lutheranism has a more traditional feel to it than most other protestant denominations. Martin Luther is the godfather of the protestant Reformation. After a terrifying thunderstorm, Luther vowed to commit his life to God, and began his religious education in 1505 A.D. Luther's experience also made him a dedicated convert. This dedication would help him spread his message and build his influence and popularity.

His study of the Word of God raised what he saw as serious errors in the Catholic church, especially the notion that anything but God's grace is sufficient to save the sinner, and make him right before God (especially the purchase of indulgences, and the Popes authority to forgive sin). Barely a decade later, on October 31, 1517 A.D., Martin Luther made history when he posted his 95 Theses on the door of the All-Saint's church in Wittenberg.

The Catholic church called Luther to attend the diet of worms in 1521 A.D. where he doubled down on his convictions. The church wouldn't budge either.

I am bound by the Scriptures I have quoted and my conscience is captive to the Word of God. I cannot and I will not retract anything, since it is neither safe nor right to go against conscience. I cannot do otherwise, here I stand, may God help me, Amen. – Martin Luther, 1521

Luther was branded a heretic and an outlaw.

His message that God alone could forgive sins, and only by faith in Christ could we be saved was a welcome breath of fresh air to an exasperated Christian population. Fed up with the church taking advantage of them, his message couldn't help but be popular among the people. Several of his contemporaries followed him and worked with him to expand his teachings.

These 'heretics' were quickly branded 'Lutherans' by the Catholic church, and the name stuck.

Lutheranism grew in Germany. By the end of 16th Century, it was the state religion in many parts of Germany, then Sweden, and Scandinavia, Hungary, Transylvania and by the 17th century arrived in US. Bishops are the heads of synods. However, The Lutheran church believes in the 'priesthood of all believers', so instead of priests, they have pastors, elders and deacons. Pastors and elders are elected by the congregation. This is an important difference to the Catholic church, where *all* of the holy orders are selected and ordained through the hierarchy system, not by the congregation.

The Lutherans boast a direct line back to Martin Luther and his break from the Catholic tradition. They represent the most orthodox and inherited tradition from Luther himself, the great reformer.

Reformers

For I am God, and there is no other; I am God, and there is none like me, declaring the end from the beginning and from ancient times things not yet done, saying, 'My counsel shall stand, and I will accomplish all my purpose,' Isaiah 46:9-10

Very soon after Luther began making waves, reformed theology took on a life of its own, spawning several clear denominational groups over time and making it one of the oldest distinct traditions, second only to Lutheranism.

Today the major Christian denominations which follow most closely in the reformed tradition are the Dutch reformed, The German reformed, the Presbyterians, the Congregationalists and the Reformed Baptists.

Reformed theology however is pervasive and its influence can be felt throughout modern Christian theology.

The reformed church began in Zurich through the efforts of Huldrich Zwingli (1484-1531).

The reformers trace their history, almost back to the beginning of the protestant Reformation.

Zwingli was a contemporary of Martin Luther, and both men were influenced by the writings of some prominent pre-Reformation thinkers, including Wycliffe and Erasmus. Luther and most of the first-generation reformers were very closely intertwined.

As both movements grew so quickly, they inevitably rubbed shoulders, to the point where many of the first-generation reformers had been influenced by, and even persuaded into The Reformation by Luther's writings.

Quite often the leaders of The Reformation heard first Luther, and were then taken under the wing of the reformers, particularly Zwingli, Farel and Bucer.

The first reformer, grew up at the Eastern base of the Swiss Alps and he began preaching in 1506. Unlike Luther, Zwingli's criticisms of the church at that time were more well received, and Zurich made many reforms under his direction. These included the removal of graven images, the declaration that priests had the right to marry, and declared transubstantiation to be unbiblical. Through Zwingli, reformed theology spread quickly through Switzerland, then Burn, Bazle, Appenzell, St Gaul, Shaflhauzen and on and on. Zwingli's base was however, in Zurich.

John Calvin (1509-1564) is the face of the reformed tradition, from whom it gets its colloquial name 'Calvinism'.

Calvin was raised in France, just north of Paris, and his father wanted him to have a good education. He studied arts and law, and eventually converted to Protestantism. Calvin was on his way from France to Spain during this time, but conflicts forced him to detour through Geneva. The town was embroiled in religious and political turmoil. A local fiery preacher, William Farel, convinced Calvin to stay in Geneva permanently. Over Calvin's life his fame and reputation as a brilliant theologian grew enormously.

Reformed theology eventually became the state religion in Geneva, and Calvin heavily influenced this achievement. Calvin's state became a hub for the development and rapid spread of his reformed theology. Calvin was a student of reformed theology, inspired by those who came before him, but hardly anyone did more to popularize and spread reformed theology throughout the world. He published his first edition of the *institutes of the Christian Religion*, while in Basel in March of 1536. This work is the cornerstone of reformed theology today.

Martin Bucer (1491–1551) was centered in Strasbourg France. He was highly influential, and yet less famous today than other reformers. Born in Schlettstadt to a poor cobbler, Bucer took his vows in 1506 – the same year as Zwingli. In 1518 he attended the Hiedelberg disputation where he was strongly convicted, and quickly left his vows in the Catholic church to join the reformers. He ended up in Strasbourg sometime around 1524 where he was present during the attempts to reconcile Luther's and Zwingli's theological perspectives on the Eucharist.

Bucer played a (noble, and difficult) role as mediator. Ultimately however the two viewpoints could not be reconciled. Bucer was also a close companion, friend and mentor to John Calvin as the two men lived together for a time and eventually became neighbors.

Presbyterians

"Set in order what remains and appoint elders in every city as I directed you, 6 namely, if any man is above reproach, the husband of one wife, having children who believe, not accused of dissipation or rebellion. 7 For the overseer must be above reproach as God's steward, not self-willed, not quick-tempered, not addicted to wine, not pugnacious, not fond of sordid gain, 8 but hospitable, loving what is good, sensible, just, devout, self-controlled, 9 holding fast the faithful word which is in accordance with the teaching, so that he will be able both to exhort in sound doctrine and to refute those who contradict." Titus 1:5-9 (NASB)

Presbyterians get their name from the term *'Presbyteros '*, from the ecclesiastical Greek, meaning 'elder', or 'one that presides over assemblies or congregations,'. Presbyterianism is one of the oldest and largest traditions in The Reformation movement. The church of Scotland, Scotland's official church is Presbyterian.

Presbyterianism was started by John Knox. Knox was born in Scotland, and educated at University of Glasgow.

Like most of the reformers, Knox was ordained into the Catholic church, then after studying the bible for himself, began to question the Catholic teachings. He was influenced by St Augustine's and St Jerome's writings and quickly left and became a passionate preacher, known for his scathing criticism of the Catholic church.

Aggravated by the abuses of Catholic theology/tradition, Knox taught in London, then fled persecution during the reign of bloody Mary – King Henry VIII's first daughter and successor, who viciously campaigned to restore Roman Catholicism in England. John Knox had a hand in the development of the 39 Articles of the Anglican religion before fleeing England and becoming a friend and contemporary of John Calvin.

From here he embraced Calvin's reformed theology and then moved back to Scotland in 1559, to start the reformed movement there within a 'Presbyterian' style of church government. In 1567 the Reformed church in Scotland was formally recognized. Presbyterianism grew quickly throughout Scotland, Holland, Ireland, and elsewhere, quickly establishing itself as a distinct and influential branch of The Reformation movement.

Eventually the church of Scotland adopted the Westminster Confession of Faith, which remains one of the key documents outlining Presbyterian reformed theology today. As with most protestant groups, Presbyterianism found its way to America early, and was very influential in early American political structure and formation.

Presbyterians follow a reformed theology, and have used the Westminster Confession of Faith to characterize their denominations view of the Bible and other crucial matters of the faith for almost their entire history.

Presbyterians reject transubstantiation, and most of the other Catholic sacraments.

Salvation is by Grace alone through faith alone in Jesus Christ.

Presbyterians affirm the central creeds of Christianity, the Nicene, Apostles and Athanasian creeds, as elaborated in the Westminster Confession of Faith.

Anglicanism

He [Jesus] said to them, "Because of your hardness of heart Moses permitted you to divorce your wives; but from the beginning it has not been this way. 9 And I say to you, whoever divorces his wife, except for immorality, and marries another woman commits adultery. Matthew 19:8-9.

There is a lot of debate about whether the Anglican church is really a 'true' protestant church, as it's often considered more of a middle ground between Catholics and Protestants. And yet, in a way, the Anglican church is probably the truest 'protestant' church of all since it was the first of the big reformers to strategically separate itself from the Catholic church. By contrast most of the first-generation protestants were either excommunicated, or forced to break away because of irreconcilable differences with the Catholic church.

The Anglican church is, basically, the church of England. The church of England separated from the Roman Catholic church through the efforts of King Henry VIII and his advisors. However, it wasn't until his daughter Queen Elizabeth I took the throne that the Anglican church really began to flourish. The church of England broke from the Catholic church during the reign of King Henry VIII. King Henry the VIII was a rather sour character. Both Henry and his eldest daughter Mary are among the most infamous rulers in British history.

So, the story goes that Henry – seeking desperately for a male heir to his throne – sought a divorce from his first wife, who provided him with 'only' a daughter, and several miscarriages (nice guy). The Pope wouldn't allow this (for political reasons, as well as theological). So, Henry exerted his authority as the King of England, and set about dissolving the Pope's authority over the affairs of the Crown. Although Henry VIII hated Martin Luther, and was not a reformer in the same sense, the origin of the church of England cannot be disconnected from the Protestant Reformation. Henry VIII's advisors, who were protestants, masterminded the plan which would allow Henry to get his divorce. Furthermore, Henry started making reforms in England that would consolidate power and wealth into the church of England.

Henry VIII was a staunch opponent of Luther's Reformation and of Luther personally. Throughout Henry's life and the short reign of his son the throne was characterized by political and religious turmoil. Henry was a money vacuum. He lived his life in almost constant debt, blowing enormous amounts of money on his lavish lifestyle. Much of this fortune was extracted from the Catholic church as he liquidated their assets across Britain. Henry was succeeded by his son, and then his first daughter Mary, who sought to abolish The Reformation and turn England back to Catholicism.

Mary was a brutal tyrant, burning no less than 300 protestants at the stake before her death merely 5 years after she took the throne. An underappreciated figure in the development of the church of England was King Henry's second daughter Elizabeth I, who would go on to become Queen Elizabeth the I. If Henry is responsible for the inauspicious circumstances surrounding the creation of the Anglican church, Queen Elizabeth is responsible for its survival.

Whilst historians almost unanimously agree that Henry's first divorce was the catalyst, it was Elizabeth's reign which brought lasting change to The Reformation in England. She restored order in the Kingdom, and brought reform to the church of England that generally satisfied the majority. The massive size and influence of the Anglican church today, has a lot to do with the historical 'fall' of the Roman Empire. Not least the eventual fall of Constantinople and the mediterranean to the Muslims also.

As the historical centerpiece of the mighty Roman Empire gradually corroded away, the West continued to flourish with England as the focal point of power and the rise of the British Empire. With the church of England as the official state church, so too did Anglicanism flourish in the West. Anglicanism adheres to the main Creeds of Christianity formed during the 3rd-5th centuries, including the Nicene and Apostles Creed and the Athanasian creed.

The Episcopalian Church

Anglicanism made its way to the United States early on in its history, and became an established with over 400 Anglican churches nationwide by 1775 A.D. At the end of the Revolutionary war, the church sought a way to reform the Anglican church, whilst being separate from the church of England (especially since those priests loyal to the crown were being imprisoned and/ or deported). This process began at the general convention, Philadelphia 1785 and culminated by the ordination of two Americans into the Anglican clergy in 1789, and the thus the Episcopalian church was born.

Anabaptists (Amish, Mennonites)

Pure and undefiled religion in the sight of our God and Father is this: to visit orphans and widows in their distress, and to keep oneself unstained by the world.

James 1:27

Anabaptists were labelled by their enemies and oppressors to identify them as heretics, and to increase persecution against them. The term roughly means 'rebaptism', because they believed their infant baptism in the Catholic church to be invalid. They advocated instead for 'believers only baptism' in adulthood, as an outward profession of one's faith. Despite their pacifism, and the persecution they suffered, anabaptists spread throughout Christendom faster than a swarm of fire ants.

On a snowy Winter's night, January 1525, in Zurich, a group of protestant believers got together, and baptized one another. This was the beginning of the Anabaptist movement. A movement not wholly unfamiliar to the majority of protestant Christianity today, yet they were considered 'radical' by the standards of the other reformers of their day. They grew out of Zwingli's reformed theology, but the anabaptists took it further. Some of the most important Anabaptists were Konrad Gretel (Zurich), Hans Denk (Bavaria), Balthasar Gubmaier (Germany). These men disagreed with Zwingli on some key issues. As Shelley states in church History:

"Most revolutionary movements produce a wing of radicals who feel called of God to reform The Reformation… calling the moderate reformers to strike even more deeply at the foundations of the old order."

These Anabaptists did what all self-respecting protestants did; they studied the Bible. They saw no biblical precedent for involving the church in the state's affairs, which included taking up arms. You see, when they declared the invalidity of their infant baptism, they immediately baptized themselves which was a crime according to most of the religious and state institutions (including the reformers). So they were:

1. Protesting against the Catholics

2. Rejecting the notion of Church and State

3. Radicalizing the protestant movement

This placed them at odds with the Catholics, Protestants and the State… which was everyone, basically.

They were heavily persecuted for this.

Anabaptists were eventually forced out of Zurich, and they attempted to gain footholds in Germany and Holland, but were met with equal amounts of resistance there. Despite The Reformations dangerous simmering cauldron of religious ultra-denominationalism, the Anabaptists stayed impressively true to their stances of non-violence and non-retaliation. Somewhere over 4000 Anabaptists were martyred during this time. Due to this persecution many fled to the United States and were taken in by the Quakers (see below) and settled in Germantown, Pennsylvania in 1683 A.D.

As Anabaptists continued to migrate to the US, they propped up in Ohio, Virginia, Indiana, Illinois, Missouri, Kansas, Nebraska, South Dakota, and the West. Today the two primary schools of Anabaptists that remain in the US are the Mennonites, and the Amish.

Anabaptists have a number of unique beliefs and many more typical protestant beliefs:

1. Believers only baptism (no infant baptism) – where they get their name (Anabaptists)

2. Strong emphasis on separation of Church and state

3. Communion (bread and wine not Christ's real blood and body)

4. Sharing of resources

5. Simple living

6. Care for the poor and widows

7. Non-violence

8. The Bible as the sole authority for faith and practice

Mennonites

The Mennonites are a branch of the Anabaptists that originated in the Netherlands and North Germany under the guidance of Menno Simmons (1496-1561). Menno was a *staunch* pacifist, despite the jarring descriptions of persecution against the Mennonites.

Sadly, in 2016, the Mennonite movement in the UK held its last official service, as its decreasing attendance forced its attendants to close the doors.

Anabaptist Mennonite Network (not a church, but an online network of anabaptists)

"The network comprises people from all over Britain and from a wide range of church backgrounds, most do not have direct historical links with Anabaptism." – AMN Dunmore East Christian Fellowship (Ireland)

Amish

Jacob Amman, a 17th-century citizen of Switzerland, was *even more radical* than the Mennonites, and took a stance on excommunication and shunning. After moving to the US, he broke away from the Mennonite church and founded the Amish. The Amish are world famous for their simple living and modest dress standards. Over time some Amish groups began to disagree as well, with some wanting to stay on the straight and narrow, and others wanting to lose the reigns just a little.

Today there are multiple flavors throughout Amish society, with some sects being a lot more open to new technology and less traditional attire, whilst others are still extremely traditional.

The Amish believe:

1. Communion twice a year

2. Foot washing

3. Separation from the world

4. Speak German and Pennsylvania Dutch

5. No electricity

6. Plain clothes akin to 17th-century European peasants

7. "Running Around" before baptism at age 17-20

8. Shunning

Anabaptists adhere to the Schleithiem Confession, put together in 1527, which gained widespread acceptance amongst Northern European Mennonites.

Another important document is the Dordrecht Confession of Faith which was composed in 1632 in the Netherlands.

Baptists

Then Jerusalem was going out to him, and all Judea and all the district around the Jordan; 6 and they were being baptized by him in the Jordan River, as they confessed their sins. Matthew 3:5-6

All you really need to know about the Baptist denomination is that they believe the only true leader of the church, is Jesus Christ. What this means is that there is little to no formal, hierarchical structure or oversight that determines what specific Baptists believe. What this means is that there is enormous variation amongst the Baptist denomination. Within the Baptist movement there are hundreds of branches and sects with a complex and storied history leading back, more or less, to The Reformation.

If you ask a committed Baptist where the Baptist church originated, they'll more than likely tell you that the Baptist church originated on the day of Pentecost, when the church originated.

They will (correctly) explain to you that from the beginning, starting with the apostles of Jesus Christ, the church was made of those who believed in Jesus Christ as their savior, who repented of their sins and were baptized in water unto the faith. Strictly speaking however, the Baptists as a denomination arose among the protestant Christians who can more reliably trace their roots back to The Reformation.

More specifically, the Baptists are descendants of the Anabaptists, the radical reformers who gained a foothold in the 1520's, early in The Reformation (themselves born out of the reformed tradition of Zwingli), but they drew influences also from the Anglican tradition too.

John Smythe is credited with starting the first 'Baptist' congregation in Amsterdam, in 1609 and the movement spread rapidly (along with many other separatist splinter groups) despite heavy persecution by the Catholic church.

However, an exact history of the origins of modern-day Baptists is not so clear cut.

Steve Weaver, Baptist Historian, argues that John Smythe likely did not found Baptists, as they exist today. He cites a 1691 work by Herculeans Collins who rejected the association with John Smythe.

Quoting Professor William Loyd Allen (in the comments), Weaver says:

"Sorting out Baptist origins is "like trying to untangle a snarled fishing line in the dark.""

John Smythe attended Cambridge University, and was ordained an Anglican. Well versed in Greek, he studied the New Testament and made one important conclusion which set him apart from his fellow Anglicans. He saw no evidence for the practice of infant baptism. He became a 'separatist' when he separated from the Anglican church (where do they come up with these names?). He then began preaching his believers baptism and gained a following. However, it is often noted that Smythe frequently changed his theology to the point where he ended up at odds with his own congregation. Eventually many of them assimilated with the Anabaptists.

Thomas Helwys, a follower of Smythe, brought the Baptist movement to London in 1612 and in 1639.

Baptism emerged in the US out of modern-day Rhode Island.

Two men, Roger Williams and John Clarke founded the Baptist movement in the United States. By the 1700's they were among the three largest denominations in the US. Today there are more Baptist groups than can be counted, with the largest being the Southern Baptist Convention (SBC).

What distinguishes the Baptist church from other denominations is their emphasis on the importance of water baptism (hence the name) for believers only. Baptists reject infant baptism, and advocate for 'full immersion', which means that an individual must be fully immersed in a body of water, otherwise it doesn't count (this was, of course, Achilles fatal mistake).

Today the largest group of Baptists in the US, the Southern Baptist Convention, emphasizes doctrinal unity and diversity in function and organization. This has allowed them to consolidate their beliefs into a more conservative doctrine. However, there is still enormous diversity across the Baptist landscape worldwide. The Baptists were among the first protestants to embrace a more 'Arminian' theology, in that they believed salvation was completely available to all who freely chose to believe it.

However, some early Baptist churches popped up preaching a more reformed theology also. Baptists today are an extremely diverse group of Christians and churches with a huge variety of individual church practices. That being said they generally all fall within the purview of traditional Christianity. They adhere to all the traditional creeds of Christianity and other protestant denominations. All Baptists today (by definition) reject infant baptism, and generally practice full immersion baptism.

Methodists

But like the Holy One who called you, be holy yourselves also in all your behavior; 16 because it is written, "You shall be holy, for I am holy." 1 Peter 1:15-16

The Wesleyan Methodist, Methodist and Holiness churches all trace their history back to John Wesley, a well-educated man who devoted his life to holiness and devout godliness. Wesleyans emphasize the born-again experience, being renewed by the Holy Spirit. There is a strong emphasis in the Wesleyan tradition on helps and services, social justice and chasing perfection. Holiness churches believe that Christians (through the power of the Holy Spirit) can be completely devoid of any sin.

By the early 18th Century, Luther's Reformation was almost a century gone by. Anglicanism was well established as were the Baptists and Congregationalists, and the religious fervor that characterized the early Reformation was being supplanted by the enlightenment.

John Wesley, the founder of the Methodist flavor of Christianity lived for 88 years (1703 – 1791). An impressive feat for the 18th Century. John Wesley and his brother Charles were born in England, and both went to Oxford. John was eventually ordained as a Deacon, and then a Priest in the church of England in 1735. John Wesley became fond of the simple notion of holiness. Inspired by some Moravians that he met, he was awestruck by their unflinching peace during a near death experience on a nearly ill-fated passage from England to the US. Upon returning to England after a disappointing missionary trip, Wesley was troubled by his own shortcomings.

It was only after hearing a sermon, reciting some of Luther's writings that he began to understand being saved completely by grace alone, through faith alone. This transformed him into an enthusiastic young evangelist. Wesley's popularity blossomed. Preaching to the poor and less fortunate, he garnered large followings who would meet most often in people's homes. By the end of the 18th century, Wesley's 'methodism' had already begun to spread throughout the United States. Wesley drew up the 25 articles of religion, modified from the Anglican's 39 articles, and began distributing it throughout his followers.

Wesley preached passionately and persuasively for almost the rest of his life, travelling allegedly hundreds of thousands of miles, preaching as far as he could go. Through skilled evangelism and passionate leaders, organized Wesleyan Christianity spread rapidly throughout the US and England, emphasizing simple holiness, practical helps, and the born-again 'experience'. Wesleyan theology came to be characterized by the daily practice of perfecting oneself. His theology of ongoing sanctification and the belief that with deliberate practice and effort Christians could eventually rid themselves completely of sinful behavior, eventually led to the holiness movement. Wesleyans affirm the apostle's creed especially, but also the Nicene and Athanasian creeds, and the Wesleyan 25 articles of religion.

Their doctrine of the three 'graces' – prevenient, justificatory, sanctifying grace emphasizes the need for living righteous, holy lives. The Wesleyans tend to be Arminian, emphasizing the free will of the believer and loss of salvation; a fairly natural consequence of their emphasis on holiness and sanctifying grace. Therefore, they believe that Jesus Christ died for all human beings, and salvation is for those who freely choose to follow Christ.

The Brethren

Since you have in obedience to the truth purified your souls for a sincere love of the brethren, fervently love one another from the heart, 1 Peter 1:22

There are two main groups of Christians who associate with the term Brethren and while distinct, have some similarities, particularly their more independent nature and non-creedal system of belief. The Brethren, or 'brothers', originally came from Germany in the late 17th century. The Reformation was in full swing, and a small group of Germans familiar with Pietists and Anabaptists committed to the New Testament as their only creed. The first minister was a man named Alexander Mack (1679-1735 A.D.).

Due to persecution (common to any protestant group which resisted state recognition), in 1723 A.D. the group was forced to make their way to the United States where they grew quickly. Several churches in the US and elsewhere today are descended from Alexander Mack and his contemporaries.

In the winter of 1827—28 A.D., four men—John Nelson Darby, Edward Cronin, John Bellett, and Francis Hutchinson, met and prayed together in Dublin, Ireland. These men met together to discuss and read the Bible together with a particular emphasis on Bible prophecy. Believing that Anglicanism, and the rise of methodism and other things had brought Christianity away from New Testament teachings. John Nelson Darby was very influential in spreading this staunchly non-creedal, highly independent church ideals.

Rather than take any particular denominational 'name' they simply saw themselves as a fellowship of brethren (brothers) who met together to worship Jesus Christ. The denomination grew quickly and gained its most prominent audience in Plymouth, UK. Today the two major branches are the Open Brethren, and the Exclusive Brethren.

The Brethren believe:

1. Simple obedience to the word of God.

2. Strong emphasis on living out and faithfully studying the word of God.

3. have a strong emphasis on preaching. They meet together every day to preach, and to read the Bible. They also regularly engage in street preaching.

4. The family unit is also central to their life and faith.

Churches Of Christ (CoC)

These are in accordance with the working of the strength of His might 20 which He brought about in Christ, when He raised Him from the dead and seated Him at His right hand in the heavenly places, 21 far above all rule and authority and power and dominion, and every name that is named, not only in this age but also in the one to come. 22 And He put all things in subjection under His feet, and gave Him as head over all things to the Church,23 which is His body, the fullness of Him who fills all in all. Ephesians 1:19-22

Churches of Christ (and similar groups) claim they are undenominational and have no central headquarters or president. The head of the church is none other than Jesus Christ. The churches of Christ movement, and many others affiliated with the 'restoration movement' from 19th century America take independence to the next level.

For Christianity, the 19th Century was a time of many ups and downs, of massive and enthusiastic revivals.

The world was changing... *fast.*

Christianity was, and still is, in the tricky situation of learning how to change with a changing world, but not in a way that undermines the basic message of Christianity. Many different ideas within Christianity were birthed during the 1800's. It was a time of great awakenings, and revivals. It was a time when many were concerned that Mainline denominations were abandoning the Bible and a solid faith, grounded in objective truth.

Many believed it was trying too hard to assimilate into the current explosion of science and technology; favoring humanistic reason and natural materialism, at the expense of trusting the Bible and God alone as our source of objective truth. Others did not see that Christianity and science were at odds, but rather, complemented one another.

Still others were concerned with Christianity's lack of enthusiasm. Old Christian institutions were being labeled by some as stagnant and lacking the fervor of first century Christianity. Many sought a more vibrant faith, one that more closely represented first century Christianity (not unlike the radical reformers during The Reformation).

One particular movement is known as the restorationist movement.

The Restoration Movement was an attempt to 'restore' Christianity to its apostolic roots (the formation of the church in the first century A.D.). They sought to restore unity in the church, believing that denominations and creeds were too divisive. They eventually came to be known simply as 'Christians', or 'disciples of Christ'.

The movement gained traction and spread rapidly across the US, and then worldwide. The largest surviving groups of this movement today have names like Christian church, Disciples of Christ and churches of Christ.

Despite the high level of autonomy, and non-creedal stance, churches of Christ churches for the most part adhere to all the central points of historical Christianity, given especially their conviction to practice church and the Christian life in accordance with the New Testament.

Pentecostalism

And when Paul had laid his hands upon them, the Holy Spirit came on them, and they began speaking with tongues and prophesying. Acts 19:6

Pentecostals are right out on the highest end of the spectrum, in terms of the revivalism that shaped the 19th Century. They take their name from their conviction that the Acts of the apostles, and the outpouring of the Holy Spirit on the day of Pentecost is how the church can, and should, be operating today. Pentecostals are the most outward proponents of the gifts of the Holy Spirit, especially healing, the gift of prophecy, and speaking in tongues.

Pentecostals charismatic and highly experiential mode of worship has influenced major portions of the Christian church, and the fruit of their unquenchable enthusiasm can be felt throughout Christendom today even amongst more conservative denominations.

Much of contemporary Christianity and enthusiasm has been heavily inspired and influenced by the fervency of Pentecostal Christianity. Pentecostalism is one of the most recent major denominations of Christianity to find its roots. It began in the early 20th Century in the United States of America, and its popularity exploded due to its irreverent, charismatic gatherings characterized by large, energetic, extended worship services and a large degree of freedom of expression.

Charles Fox Parham was a teacher at Bethel Bible College, where the first instance of speaking in tongues was recorded. The movement quickly spread to Houston, Texas.

William J Seymore, a student of Charles Fox Parham led the Azuza St Revival in Los Angeles. He was the first to advocate that speaking in tongues was the surest evidence of being filled with the Holy Spirit.

Initially the Pentecostal Movement was met with significant backlash from the mainline US denominations, and so the majority of Pentecostal believers were forced to separate, and form their own denomination. Over time however, the spark of Pentecostal enthusiasm continued to spread. Its popularity continued to grow, and by the mid-20th Century Pentecostal beliefs had made their way into other denominations, especially the Roman Catholic church.

The defining characteristic of Pentecostals is their teaching that the baptism of the Holy Spirit is a secondary experience that follows salvation, and is necessary (or at least highly conducive) to empower the believer to be highly effective in their ministry. Most importantly is the role of the 'gifts of the Holy Spirit' and how they are expressed today, especially the gifts of 'tongues', 'healing' and 'prophecy'.

For the vast majority of Pentecostals, the gift of 'speaking in tongues', is interpreted as the ability to speak in a 'heavenly language' unintelligible to humans, but is communicated through the Holy Spirit for the *edification of the believer* ', and the building up of the church. However, many also acknowledge the gift as describing the phenomenon of individuals spontaneously speaking in a known human language the given individual has never heard, or learned. This is consistent with how the gift was manifested by Peter on the day of Pentecost.

And they were all filled with the Holy Spirit and began to speak in other tongues as the Spirit gave them utterance...6 And at this sound the multitude came together... 7 And they were amazed and astonished, saying, "Are not all these who are speaking Galileans? 8 And how is it that we hear, each of us in his own native language? Acts 2:4-7

Furthermore, there is an enormous variety of interpretations of the Spiritual Gifts, even within Pentecostalism/charismatic Christianity. Besides this, significant portions of Pentecostal Christianity are known for other 'signs and wonders', including commonly a phenomenon known as 'being slain in the Spirit', which involves an individual involuntarily exhibiting some outburst of behavior, which can be anything from convulsions, to bursts of laughter, or abundant and outward feelings of immense joy and ecstasy. Many

Pentecostals traditionally view speaking in tongues as the first evidence of being 'baptized by the Holy Spirit', and argue that the gift is freely available to all who *earnestly* seek it.

Others are more conservative, and adhere to Paul's admonition in 1 Corinthians 12 that the gifts are distributed among the believers at the Holy Spirits discretion, all are given a gift, but tongues are only one of a number of possible gifts. Other gifts of the spirit include the gift of healing, prophecy, interpretation, teaching, apostleship, helps/service, understanding/wisdom, and more. Many Pentecostals believe that there is a special gift of healing given to some, but that all Christians can pray for healing and miracles.

*In general, virtually **all** Christians accept that anyone can call on Jesus Christ, and pray for healing and wellness. But the belief that the 'gift of healing' especially exists as a 'gift of the Holy Spirit' and is still active today is unique to Pentecostals.*

Some believe further that God is willing to heal (literally) anyone, and everyone who prays for it, and that failure to see healing is based on some other factor, such a lack of faith.

Another important aspect of Pentecostal theology is that of prophecy. This can take many forms, but in general is manifest as a particular 'word' for either a congregation, an individual believer, or sometimes even directed toward entire geographic regions, or whole countries.

Many also believe that any Christian can be moved by the Spirit to prophesy if they seek it out. Prophecy, in the typical Pentecostal sense is believed to be a direct imparting of special knowledge from God, prompted by the Holy Spirit.

Some major Pentecostal churches, like Bethel for instance have stirred controversy for some of their more extreme practices, for example the bizarre and recent phenomenon known as 'grave sucking'.

Besides their views on the baptism, and the gifts of the Holy Spirit, Pentecostals in general hold to the same fundamental historic Christian doctrines, as the majority of other protestants. However, the ecstatic appeal of many areas of Pentecostal practice may have a tendency to overpower the more biblical and straightforward aspects of the Gospel.

The vast majority of Pentecostals are loving, joyful, enthusiastic and sincere followers of Jesus Christ who put the Bible as their sole authority of faith and practice, as sincerely as any other red-blooded protestant.

Many individuals within the Pentecostal/Charismatic Movement have been hugely successful in their major missionary campaigns, especially in third world nations.

Non-Denominational Churches

And now these three remain: faith, hope and love. But the greatest of these is love.

1 Corinthians 13:13 (NIV)

For a lot of people Christian denominations are seen as divisive and sectarian; denominations hold Christians back from the truly united ideal they envision in New Testament Christianity. As the idea of different Christian denominations in the 20th Century emerged in recent years as something to be ashamed of, an increasing number of churches have popped up and formed independent congregations. These churches are not associated with any established denominations and, as a result, have proven to be extremely popular.

Many non-denominational churches represent some of the largest mega-churches in the United States, with multiple 'campuses' spread across the country. Modern non-denominational churches are motivated more by a desire for independence from some organizational body or higher authority (other than God).

This independence gives them freedom to innovate, and to be able to adapt and respond quickly to a changing culture. For this reason, non-denominational churches tend to be quite popular. They are not shackled by tradition or complicated confessions.

There are four main reasons non-denominational churches have been so attractive, especially to younger generations:

1. The lack of a denominational tie means these churches do not have the difficult challenge of explaining to young people why they should be interested in centuries old religious confessions or creeds. They adopt inclusive, welcoming titles like 'community church' that send a message that you are welcome here

2. Their often energetic, contemporary style of worship and order of service

3. A talented and commanding preacher who is well spoken and likeable. Many non-denominational churches are most recognizable by their senior pastor. These pastors often preach a message that is very applicable to our everyday lives and experiences

4. These churches are often extremely well organized, and high quality in everything from the runtime, to the building itself. Non-denominational churches are often very clean, large, new buildings with many extras – groups and weekly activities of every imagining, many have professional on-site cafe's, child care facilities, enormous car parks, and many paid staff, especially ushers who aid newcomers in navigating their enormous campuses.

Another reason that these churches are so popular is the widespread appeal of their teachings. Modern non-denominational churches have adopted a style of church and worship which has placed emphasis on simple, digestible matters of the Christian Faith which don't rouse significant disagreement or controversy amongst Christians. Their message is generally quite simple, the world needs to know the 'love of Jesus'. Which is a good message. But it leaves a lot to the imagination.

One issue that non-denominational churches have is too often being a synonym for non-offensive. One reason that different church denominations exist, is because whilst the essential doctrines of Christianity are relatively straightforward, some of the Bible is more challenging. Not only that but denominations can arise over the emphasis of certain doctrines over others, or what parts are more important.

In other words, if your church prides itself in being non-denominational, it's probably because that church theologically detours around the dirty details and nuance of Christian theology. The paradox of being a church independent of a traditional denomination, is that while you're at liberty to emphasize your trust in the Bible alone as God's Word, it also affords substantial creative license in the development of your individual church's beliefs.

With no doctrinal standards, or centuries of theological elaboration, modern independent churches are at liberty, to take as many liberties as they like with God's Word.

That being said, most non-denominational churches accept and preach the main historic beliefs of Protestant Christianity. Due to their more energetic style of worship and living, non-denominational churches are also often very attractive to individuals who lean more toward a charismatic/Pentecostal faith, with the large, concert style worship sessions being an opportunity for those seeking a more experiential style of worship.

The Fringe

The following are a list of a few groups which are considered more on the fringe of Christian orthodoxy and are commonly regarded as not true Christianity by large groups within more mainstream protestant denominations (especially more conservative, or evangelical denominations) and Catholicism.

There is no doubt many more than what I've listed here, but the following are quite prominent and well-known, especially within Christianity.

Word of Faith/Prosperity Gospel

I'm pushing my luck by not calling out the prosperity Gospel as a straight up heresy. But I want to emphasize that prosperity Gospel teachers, so far as I am aware still teach the fundamentals of the Christian faith, at least in theory.

The prosperity gospel has been given multiple names including, 'the Charismatic Movement', 'the health and wealth gospel', 'name and claim it', and others, but this movement is simply based on two overarching, but related ideas. This movement teaches that, apart from salvation and heaven,

God will give us abundant blessings both for: Healing and Prosperity... *if we have enough faith.*

More importantly, is that most of the leaders of this movement have been able to amass their stupendous fortunes by promising healing and prophetic words for their followers *in exchange for an admission ticket,* or in the form of donations because: *'With what you generously give, God will repay even more'.*

Seventh Day Adventists

Seventh Day Adventists grew out of the 'Second Great Awakening' of the 19th Century. The group was founded by William Miller, in the 1830's. Miller considered himself a prophet of God, but he turned out to be very wrong. Miller surmised that Christ was returning in 1844, based on his understanding of Daniel 8:14:

He said to me, "For 2,300 evenings and mornings; then the holy place will be properly restored."

He quickly gained a large, devout following who lived with fervent expectation for the return of Christ. As you might have guessed, it didn't happen. This led to what's known as 'the Great Disappointment'.

Adventists:

1. Accept the infallibility of the Bible

2. Believe in the trinity (but their history is controversial, they didn't always).

3. They have a statement of beliefs which appears to be basically in line with Christianity

4. Have about 20 million Members worldwide

By far their most distinguishing beliefs today are:

1. The imminent return of Christ (Advent) which, for what it's worth, is not particularly distinct from traditional protestant theology.

2. The key point though is their emphasis on the 'imminence', which seems to be a throwback from their original belief in Christ's return in 1844.

3. They (very sensibly) don't set any specific date, but are generally expecting Christ's return 'any minute now'.

Other protestants put less emphasis on the 'when' of Christ's return and more on the 'readiness'. The Bible clearly explains that Christ will come 'like a thief in the night', and no one will know, until it happens (then *everyone* will know at once). There adherence to the 'sabbath' day of rest (Saturday, the *seventh day* of the week), as opposed to Sunday, which other Christians tend to associate with Christ's resurrection.

There are several issues with the Adventist church:

1. Their initial rejection of the trinity, which appeared to be adopted later, in an effort to maintain orthodoxy with traditional Christianity

2. The denomination was entirely born out of the teachings of a demonstrated false prophet (Ellen White, more so than William Miller), and still holds them in high regard

3. Their belief that something specific did happen in 1844, if not the second-coming of Christ. This seems to be an attempt to save face in the presence of a blatant falsehood.

4. The movement was kicked along by the desperate attempts to salvage a false prophecy by advocating for even more spurious and unverifiable nonsense.

5. The legalistic nature of their doctrines. For example, their adherence to the 'sabbath', and their insistence on 'healthy eating.'

Friends (Quakers)

This movement started with George Fox in the 17th century. Dissatisfied with Christianity as it was, Fox sought an 'authentic Christianity'.

After much soul searching (but apparently not much Bible study) Fox claimed a direct encounter with Christ. Fox's followers first gathered into an organized meeting in 1667, which became regular meetings. From this time on the church grew. Like so many others, Fox's followers also experienced persecution both in Europe, and when they first emigrated to the US.

Quakers believe that *all* humans possess an inner light. Those who are receptive, and earnestly seek God's prompting can hear directly from him. This is their mode of ministry in the church, where individuals share and speak as the Holy Spirit enables them.

Quakers are distinguished by a number of characteristics too:

1. Men and women ought to seek out God, and respond to His prompting, and they will receive more 'light'

2. God can speak directly to the heart of a believer

3. Strong anti-slavery stance (commendable)

4. Gifts of the Holy Spirit – as guided by the inner light

5. Simple living and dress

6. No paid clergy, unstructured, spontaneous style of worship

7. No sacraments

8. Belief that 'God is in everyone'

9. Very open to a variety of experiences and personal beliefs

There is still a core in this denomination which believes in the Christian God, and accepts the fundamentals of Christian belief, even if they are extremely open minded, and have an unorthodox method of worship, to say the least.

Unorthodoxies And Venerations

The following groups share a couple of important characteristics:

1. They generally consider themselves 'Christian' denominations, or at least, they adopt the use of the term Christian because it serves a useful evangelistic purpose

2. They all deny at least one of the established, critical doctrines of Christianity, most often the doctrine of the trinity, or the divinity of Jesus Christ

3. They were all established no earlier than the 19th Century

4. Typically, either humans are elevated in some way to some level of higher spiritual authority, or God (or Jesus Christ) is cast down to something less than all-powerful, eternal and everlasting

In general, each one individually considers itself the *only* 'true' denomination, and regard other groups not within their purview to be false religions. Along the same vein, *All* of them are considered by *all* traditional Christian denominations as cults or heresies.

The Church of Jesus Christ of the Latter-Day Saints (Mormons)

The church of Jesus Christ of the Latter-Day Saints, also known as the Mormons, is a significant church started by Joseph Smith in the 19th Century, in New York City. According to legend, way back in the 4th Century (around the time the canon of the Bible was being formalized), an angel named 'Mormon' wrote a 'sacred' book on golden plates (which is absolutely the most normal and sensible material you would use to inscribe a large amount of religious text).

The angel Mormon buried this book in what is now modern-day New York where it remained for almost two thousand years. Then in 1822 the angel's son (also an angel), came to a man named Joseph Smith, in a vision and told him about the sacred writings. The angel wanted Smith to translate the book.

Smith allegedly discovered the book in 1827, and immediately set about translating (with the help of God) the text of the golden plates into English. This translation was published in 1830.

Mormonism grew quickly, but was also heavily persecuted. Sadly, Joseph Smith and his brother were jailed, and eventually murdered whilst in prison.

Brigham Young quickly succeeded Smith, shepherded in many of the remaining Mormon's and eventually migrated them to Utah where they *founded* (seriously!) Salt Lake City – I'm sure this is common knowledge in Utah. It is from this home base that Mormonism grew steadily into the 16 million strong membership that it is today.

According the Mormon faith, the Book of Mormon, and the Bible are both equally divine and authoritative, however the Book of Mormon is essentially 'higher' than the Bible in that it contains corrections and 'higher' truths. Mormons also hold two other texts as equal in authority with the Bible and the Book of Mormon:

1. Doctrine and Covenants – rolling release updates to Christian doctrine.

2. The Pearl of Great Price (which adds to and clarifies points which were 'lost' from the Bible)

These writings are elevated to the same level of authority as the Bible because they were written by 'prophets' (mostly they were written by Joseph Smith) and believed to be divinely inspired. Smith believed that Mormonism was the restoration of 'true' Christianity, and that all other denominations had gone astray. There are several issues that exclude Mormonism as a legitimate Christian denomination. They have a number of beliefs which are clearly not taught in the Bible, and are particularly serious:

1. They believe that God the Father was once a man

2. That Jesus and Satan are brothers (i.e. Jesus is not eternal, omniscient, a member of the trinity)

3. That the Bible contains significant errors

4. The problem with this is that the only real basis for trusting in the God of the Bible, is in having confidence that His word is true.

5. If the Bible contains errors, then why should we bother to trust it at all?

And why should we then bother to trust the word of a man who followed Jesus by almost 2000 years, and claimed that *his* book was the correct one, and fixed all the problems in the Bible?

The Book of Mormon logically undermines its own authority, by undermining the Bible's.

Despite my sarcasm, I should note that I bear no ill-will towards individual Mormons, or individuals of other cults more generally. I am acquainted with more than one person who is a member of the LDS church, whom I know to be really nice (and very intelligent) people.

Just because I believe that the LDS church is not a Christian church, does not mean I think they are bad, or weird. The challenge is that they believe they are, but the rest of Christianity doesn't, and the Bible agrees.

Jehovah's Witnesses

Jehovah's Witnesses were founded in 1872, when Charles Taze Russel began the 'student society'. Today this group has over 20 million attendees' worldwide with over 8.5 million evangelists. Charles Taze Russel sprung out of the 'Adventist' movement (see 'Seventh Day Adventists' above), already known for their controversial and failed messianic predictions of the second coming of Jesus Christ.

Russel's teachings were even more obscure, moving away from the clear teaching of the Bible, denying most especially that Jesus was God, and denying the doctrine of the trinity. Following the failed predictions of the Adventists, Taze made his own new predictions that Christ was *actually* returning in 1914... unfortunately World War I started instead. Charles died in 1916 and was succeeded by Joseph Rutherford in 1917 who was instrumental in the growth and institutionalization of the Witnesses in the coming decades.

Rutherford introduced significant changes to the doctrines and teachings of Russel, including the additions of (bizarre?) predictions, such as that Abraham and Isaac would be resurrected in 1925. In 1931 Rutherford Changed the name to "Jehovah's Witnesses." Jehovah's Witnesses are a tight knit organization that runs like a well-oiled machine. They have millions of publications in print including their famous, regularly published 'Watchtower'.

They are probably most famous however, for their extremely dedicated door-to-door evangelization efforts whereby, according to britannica.com:

Each congregation has an assigned territory and each Witness a particular neighborhood to canvass. Great precautions are taken to keep records of the number of visits, return calls, Bible classes, and books and magazines distributed.

A lot could be said about Jehovah's Witnesses.

There is a more distinctive 'cultyness' about their organization. This is seen in their long list of isolating behavior and practices including, but not limited to:

1. Meticulously efficient record keeping and organizational structure

2. Their tendency towards exclusivism

3. Disavowing secular government

4. Strict code of ethics

5. Refusing military service and

6. Non-participation in all traditional Christian holiday's such as Christmas and Easter

Expectation of virtually total obedience to the teachings of the watch tower, and little to no tolerance for personal opinion on matters of biblical understanding, and watch tower publications, at least

Publishing their own, exclusive, version of the Bible (with subtle, but crucial differences to the Christian Bible) and disregarding *all* other versions completely

There's something very exclusive and overbearing how they practice their faith. More seriously however, what clearly identifies Jehovah's Witnesses as a non-Christian sect is their denial of:

1. The trinity

2. Bodily return of Jesus Christ

3. The divinity of Jesus Christ

4. The divinity and personhood of the Holy Spirit

For what it's worth, Jehovah's Witness *do* clearly teach their belief that "Jesus is not Almighty God."

However, they very cleverly word these beliefs with statements which may easily confuse or mislead the careless observer.

For example, they state their belief that Jesus is "son of god", and that "therefore", they are Christians.

But this misses the key (and obvious) point that Christians believe *Jesus is God*, the second person of the trinity.

Christian Scientists

Christian Science has virtually nothing to do with actual science, or Christianity for that matter.

Despite the insistence that their teachings are "rooted in the Bible" (just ask them, they'll tell you).

This belief system was founded by Mary Baker Eddy who allegedly experienced a healing event (although this is controversial) in 1866 based on her reading of the Bible. She then *allegedly* dedicated herself to Bible study and eventually…

"Christian Science flowed out of an inspired understanding of the Bible, which illumined the divine laws behind spiritual healing." – Official Website

Eddy's esoteric spirituality was initially very appealing, and the group gained significant adherents, finances and influence throughout the early 20th century but has been in sharp decline since the 1980's.

Throughout the 20th century Christian Scientists set up multiple buildings called "Church of Christ, Scientist" (that's the actual name) beginning with the 'mother church' called "The First Church of Christ, Scientist, Christian Science Centre" in Boston, Massachusetts which is still the headquarters for Christian Science today.

The central theme of Christian Science is a strong emphasis on healing through prayer. Christian Science claims that sickness and ailments don't really exist, but are actually just an illusion, the consequence of not being close to God.

Reality is God's Kingdom (apparently the Bible tells us this).

The key to healing is in understanding this higher truth and blindly believing it regardless of any evidence to the contrary, no matter how plain and straightforward. This healing is achieved through prayer, with the assistance of 'qualified' practitioners (who are not medically trained professionals), which brings us closer to 'father-mother, and divine manhood'.

The only illusion here, is the feigned connection between the God of Christian Science and the God of the Bible, despite childishly elementary differences. Christian Science smacks of new age mysticism. The way its adherents describe their faith has a characteristic vagueness to it, like their taking ordinary sentences, and then rearranging them like puzzles pieces. More importantly though, Christian Science:

1. Denies the trinity

2. Denies the existence of matter despite their being absolutely no hint of this in the Bible (although it is a popular theory in metaphysics), and plenty of biblical evidence to the contrary like Genesis 1 – God made the world…

3. Incorrectly believes that suffering is caused by 'separation from God', when in fact suffering and separation from God are both caused by original sin

4. Has an extremely vague view of Jesus, and it's unclear exactly what they believe about Him (although it's quite clear that it is wrong)

Mary's Baker Eddy's theology was heavily influenced and inspired by other non-Christian philosophies including homeopathy. The insistence of prayer healing becomes a lot more serious when it comes to their historic practice of refusing any and all medical attention to the detriment, and death, of their followers… *and their followers' children.*

Denominations Wrap-Up

One of the most challenging things when looking at denominations and especially the cults, is knowing how many probably perfectly well-meaning, and very kind and friendly people inhabit these various beliefs, no matter how barking mad some of them are. It's hard being so critical of belief systems full of very nice, friendly people. But this is the nature of finding truth.

If something is not true, it doesn't matter how nice it sounds, or how nice the people are who believe it, it's still untrue. In the end, what is most important is finding a church that believes the Bible, teaches the Bible and has a passion to reach the lost.

Most denominations exist because they sought to restore the Bible to its rightful place as the sole authority for Christian Faith and practice. Though it is not considered a salvation issue (i.e. you can still be a Christian and believe in extra revelation) hopefully you notice a common theme that how closely a group or denomination holds to biblical authority often dictates whether they are considered a legit denomination, a fringe, or an outright cult.

At the heart of this issue is that anything that does not come from the Bible runs the risk of becoming an authority unto itself. This often has serious consequences. The real issue arises as the religious group (often gradually) comes to raise the level of authority of one or more individuals up to, and even over the authority of the Bible.

Generally speaking, the more closely and exclusively a particular denomination stands on the infallibility and sufficiency of the bible, the more theologically and morally conservative that denomination tends to be. Or to put it another way, the less emphasis placed on the bible as the sole authority of truth and practice for the Christian faith, the further the focus of the denomination shifts away from the Gospel of Jesus Christ, towards something else.

"As we have said before, so I say again now, if any man is preaching to you a gospel contrary to what you received, he is to be accursed!" Galatians 1:9

The modern sensitivities of many Christians today lead many to view the Middle Ages as a less civilized time. They seem to have had a kind of primitive tendency toward violence, especially in the handling of The Reformation by both the Roman Catholics and the reformers. Tensions were super high, and wars were fought over different theological viewpoints. This might seem really strange to us in a more 'civilized' age.

Today we pride ourselves in our civilized government, and our ability to solve disputes in a more peaceful way.

It's worth noting however, the reformers would've balked at this attitude. What we see today as a more civilized approach to discussion, the reformers would've seen us as nothing more than lukewarm and indifferent. More importantly, The Reformation almost certainly would not have gained traction in the way it did, if it were not for their passion and zeal. The reformers believed with all their heart that they were rescuing the Western world from corruption and damnation. They preached with a passion, and were willing to fight tooth and nail for what they saw as a purpose and goal so much greater than themselves. Their enthusiasm and passion were infectious, and highly instrumental in winning souls to their cause.

Similarly, from the Catholic point of view, the reformers were riotous upstarts of the highest order. Their alarming rise in popularity posed a serious threat not only to their accumulated power and influence, but to the established orthodoxy of the Christian church. These 'cult' reformers were leading away entire towns from the 'one true church' and straight into the fires of hell. Churches today are hemorrhaging Christians, as every year millions of impressionable teens fall victim to selfish worldly philosophies and modern ideologies. Evolution teaches them that they are mere accidents of accidental chemical reactions. They have no purpose and no meaning, and nothing they do matters. Those there is no value in human life. Yet we wonder why there are so many murders and school shootings!

Social justice ideas teach them that they are broken, fragile, pathetic and that only the government has the power to save them. One of the great challenges of Christianity in the 21st Century is lighting fires in the hearts of the Christian population to spread the message of Christianity. Ask any pastor today anywhere in the world what they most desire of their congregation. I guarantee for most the answer is a more passionate, zealous congregation, more willing to rise up and preach boldly the word of God.

In many evangelical circles today, especially in larger more populous Christian circles, there is an increasing emphasis on ecumenism, a push for a form of Christian unity. The problem is this *denies* that Christianity is already united fully under Christ. In an ideal world, all Christians everywhere (and all humans for that matter) would have a perfect understanding of scripture and its ordinances for the Christian life. All Christians would be in complete agreement, and know the full truth of every doctrinal matter there is to know about, and there would be complete unity in faith. Most importantly, everybody would know and trust that Jesus Christ is real, and He is our Savior.

Indeed, the Bible says:

The Lord is not slow about His promise, as some count slowness, but is patient toward you, not wishing for any to perish but for all to come to repentance. 2 Peter 3:9

But this is not an ideal world. This is a fallen world, and the church is run by human beings. So, inevitably, there is disagreement. Denominations exist because truth is important, and no single human, or denomination is the gatekeeper of truth, only God.

Taking denominations away from Christianity is to make a Christianity for children. The idea of all Christians the world over coming to a single, unified, orthodox catechism of beliefs is at best a total fantasy, at worst an extremely dangerous and terrifying notion. This suggests that at some point mortal, imperfect Christians will have claim to the ultimate truth of Christianity and all discussion will hence be silenced.

I totally understand the sentiment that we just want all Christians to 'get along'... but Christians with different theological opinions getting along and respecting one another is not the same as declaring a single universal denomination with a single set of beliefs. If such a set of beliefs could exist, it would be shallow inclusiveness beyond recognition, and theologically worthless. This is a Christianity where people no longer sit with each other, only next to each other; a Christianity where there are no arguments, because there is no talking. It is a place where discussion dies, where individuality is not tolerated, where freedom of expression is marginalized, not in favor of group think, but something worse... no think.

As soon as we start putting all the focus of Christianity on some idealized form of 'unity', we are all implicitly agreeing to stop seeking the truth, and stop talking about the deeper issues. Many people today, especially many Christians view Christian denominations with cynicism, as something divisive that Christians should be ashamed of.

But could it be seen as a something much more noble, with a noble history, and a noble cause?

Do Christian denominations actually divide Christianity, or do they actually bring them together?

Denominations have created a platform that brings Christians together under a set of surprisingly clear, unified beliefs, like a blanket that spreads out and captures us all together under Christ. Denominations are not the result of divisive Christians stubbornly staking their claim to orthodoxy, to the exclusion of others, but instead are the natural and almost inevitable result of continued discussion and time itself. Denominations are an expression of the massively trans-cultural, ethnic, geographical and ideological influence of Christianity. The Christian denominational landscape is a celebration of the freedom that we have in Christ to study and understand the word of God for ourselves, and yet still remain 'one in Christ'. And that's something I cannot be more grateful for.

"I hope no reader will suppose that 'mere' Christianity is here put forward as an alternative to the creeds of existing communions...It is more like a hall out of which doors open into several rooms...it is in the rooms, not in the hall, that there are fires and chairs and meals. The hall is a place to wait in... not a place to live in." – C.S. Lewis, Mere Christianity.

Every generation experiences change.

But sometimes you sense you're in the midst of truly radical change, the kind that happens only every few centuries. Increasingly, I think we're in such a moment now. Those of us in in Western culture who are over thirty years of age were born into a culture that could conceivably still be called Christian. In America, people who are churchless (having no church affiliation) will soon eclipse the churched. In addition, 48% of Millennials (born between 1984-2002) can be called post-Christian in their beliefs, thinking and worldview.

Perhaps the change we're seeing around us might one day be viewed on the same level as what happened to the church after Constantine's conversion or after the invention of the printing press. Whatever the change looks like when it's done, it will register as a seismic shift from what we've known.

So, what will the future church be like? And how should you and I respond?

Making predictions can be a dangerous thing, maybe even a bit ridiculous. We should be passionate about the mission of the church, and knowing Jesus Christ is in charge should give us a positive glimmer for the future. However, I urge you to consider my predictions as if written with a pencil and not in ink. I do not claim to be a profit, I am only stating the following based on my hope for the future and my ultimate hope in Christ. While no one's *really* sure of what's ahead, talking about it at least allows us to position our churches for impact in a changing world.

A Balanced View of the Church

There is a pivotal text that provides answers found in Ephesians 4:11-16:

"So, Christ himself gave the apostles, the prophets, the evangelists, the pastors and teachers, to equip his people for works of service, so that the body of Christ may be built up until we all reach unity in the faith and in the knowledge of the Son of God and become mature, attaining to the whole measure of the fullness of Christ." Then we will no longer be infants, tossed back and forth by the waves, and blown here and there by every wind of teaching and by the cunning and craftiness of people in their deceitful scheming. Instead, speaking the truth in love, we will grow to become in every respect the mature body of him who is the head, that is, Christ. From him the whole body, joined and held together by every supporting ligament, grows and builds itself up in love, as each part does its work.

So, what's likely ahead for the future church? Here is my hope:

1. The potential to gain is still greater than the potential to lose. Every time there is a change in history, there's potential to gain and potential to lose. *Why?* As cynical as some might be, and this is very understandably, the church's future, we have to remind ourselves is the idea of Jesus and not ours. It will survive our missteps and whatever cultural trends happen around us. We certainly don't always get things right, but Christ has an incredible history of pulling together Christians in every generation to share his love for a broken world. As a result, the reports of the church's death are greatly exaggerated.

2. Churches that love their model more than the mission will die. That said, many individual congregations and some entire denominations won't make it. The difference will be between those who cling to the mission and those who cling to the model. When the car was invented, it quickly took over from the horse and buggy. Horse and buggy manufacturers were relegated to secondary status and many went under, but human transportation actually exploded. Suddenly average people could travel at a level they never could before. The mission is travel. The model is a buggy, or car, or motorcycle, or jet. The model always shifts.... moving from things like 8 tracks, cassettes and CDs to MP3s and now streaming audio and video. Companies that show innovation around the mission (Apple, Samsung) will always beat companies that remain devoted to the method (Kodak). Churches need to stay focused on the mission (leading people into a growing relationship with Jesus) and be exceptionally innovative in our model.

3. The gathered church is here to stay. Read the comments on any church leader blog and you would think that some Christians believe the best thing to do is to give up on Christian gatherings of any kind. While some will leave, it does not change the fact that the church has *always* gathered because the church is inherently communal. Additionally, what we can do gathered together far surpasses what we can do alone. Which is why there will always be an organized church of some form. Christians will always gather together to do more than we ever could on our own. We will gather often, read the Scriptures, worship intently, pray fervently, be led by servants, live authentically, and honor the Sacraments. For sure, we will continue to be creative and inventive but not at the expense of the ancient structure which has transcended all generations for over 2000 years.

4. Community - The concept of a community of believers is essential to God's plan for His church. The Bible uses the following words as apt descriptors for the church: people, body, household, and family. It's obvious from Scripture that God wants His people to grow and mature within a community of unity and togetherness. It was never God's intent for His followers to practice their faith in a vacuum away from other believers. New converts need the fellowship and community of a body of other believers to truly become all that God has for them to be.

5. Consumer Christianity will die and a more selfless discipleship will emerge. Consumer Christianity asks *What can I get from God?* It asks, *What's*

in it for me? That leads us to evaluate our church, our faith, our experience and each other according to our preferences and whims. In many respects, even many critics of the church who have left have done so under the pull of consumer Christianity because 'nothing' meets their needs. All of this is opposite to the Gospel, which calls us to die to ourselves—to lose ourselves for the sake of Christ. As the church reformats and repents, a more authentic, more selfless church will emerge. Sure, we will still have to make decisions about music, gathering times and even some distinctions about what we believe, but the tone will be different. When you're no longer focused on yourself and your viewpoint, a new tone emerges.

6. Worship Service will become more about what we give than what we get. The death of consumer Christianity will change our gatherings. Our gatherings will become less about us and more about Jesus and the world he loves. Rather than a gathering of the already-convinced, the churches that remain will be decidedly outsider-focused. And word will be supplemented with deeds. In the future church, being right will be less important than doing right. Sure, that involves social justice and meeting physical needs, but it also involves treating people with kindness, compassion in everyday life and attending to their spiritual wellbeing. This is the kind of outward focus that drove the rapid expansion of the first century church. We can get excited to be part of a group of churches that has, at its heart, the desire to create churches of unchurched people who love to attend. While the expression of what that looks like may change, the intent will not. Source: https://careynieuwhof.com/10-predictions-about-the-future-church-and-shifting-attendance-patterns/

7. Commitment - This passage also points out that a tangible commitment to the local church is what the Lord intends from His people. He doesn't want only a select few of His followers to do their part while the majority of other church attendees sit on the sidelines uninvolved. The church is at its best when every believer is devoted to the mission of His church.

8. The church will return to wonder and awe. The churches that embrace the miraculous nature of God will see the most growth and have the most influence in the future. Good preaching, trendy stage sets, and clever videos will not be enough in the next ten years because people want to see God intervene more and more in the affairs of the people with miracles and healings. Sound theology must prevail, and we must not return to our sloppy religious tendencies. We must embrace the mysterious and risky nature of God and not be afraid of wonder and awe. While the Holy Spirit may be unpredictable, the results are always predictable – people will find God, people will be healed, and people will discover real truth and freedom.

9. Spiritual Maturity - God designed His church to be a catalyst for spiritual growth. The language here uses a familiar visual illustration of a child growing into maturity. This truth, of course, must include the idea that there has been a "new birth-experience" (John 3:7), and so reaching people for Christ is intrinsically involved. Therefore, it is imperative for the church to be about the task of seeing people come to Christ and helping them grow towards maturity in Christ.

10. Service - Serving the Lord must be at the center of every local church's programming and functions. This passage is clear that God wants each believer to actively serve Him by ministering to others in and through their local church. Obviously, salvation, when a person puts their faith and trust in Christ, is when the process of service begins. Scripture also presents the idea that every believer is the recipient of God-given spiritual gifts, which are God's enabling ability to effectively serve Him (1 Corinthians 12 and Romans 12:3-8). It was never God's intent for the church to be a "spectator sport" where people show up on Sunday mornings to watch others perform. God expects every Christ-follower to use their natural abilities and spiritual gifts to faithfully serve Him.

11. Growth - The end result of the local church operating as Christ intended is that the church will grow — both spiritually and numerically. Growing churches do not depend upon some man-made plan or program. The Bible is clear that God wants each one of His people to intentionally, actively, and faithfully share their faith with others. However, evangelism is to be done through the church where those who come to Christ can grow in Him and also participate in the church's mission. Attendance will no longer drive engagement; engagement will drive attendance. Currently, many churches try to get people to attend, hoping it drives engagement. In the future, that will flip. The engaged will attend, in large measure because only the engaged will remain. If you really think about engagement driving attendance, it is exactly what has fueled the church at its best moments throughout history. It's an exciting shift.

12. Looking at Truth - If it's new, it's probably not truth. If its truth, it's probably not new.

In 2005, the United Church of Christ became the first mainline Protestant denomination to officially embrace gay marriage. They expected this progressive stance to result in a growth boom. In 2006, with great optimism, the UCC announced the ambition to plant more than 1,600 new congregations by 2021. Over that 15-year period, however, the denomination's membership declined by more than 40 percent; 60 percent of its congregations now have fewer than 50 people; and in 2021 it sold its national headquarters to pay bills.

This story shouldn't surprise us. This is the story of mainline Protestantism over the past 60 years. In 1960, the seven mainline denominations boasted 30 million members. Now they have 13 million. Writing at the Institute on Religion and Democracy, John Lomperis observes, "churches that . . . reject clear biblical teaching on sexual morality can expect dramatic, long-term, and irreversible membership decline."

The numbers don't lie: theological liberalism leads to stagnation and decay. Whatever future the American church has, it'll lie in the hands of those who embrace historic Christian orthodoxy.

https://hegetsus.com/en/articles/jesus-was-fed-up-with-politics-too?
gclsrc=3p.ds&msclkid=4ad522be18f5151ac07a44e44f709b84&utm_source
=bing&utm_medium=cpc&utm_campaign=LERMA%7CHAVEN%7CHGU
%7CNONBRAND%7CGOOGLE%7CSEARCH%7CNAT%7CRESCON
%7C&utm_term=jesus%20and%20politics%20in%20the
%20bible&utm_content=Politics

We must hold more firmly than ever to the gospel!

The gospel is still faithful and true. To reach the lost, they must hold more firmly than ever to the gospel, find stability on its rock-solid ground, and move forward engaging the culture.

In Jesus' time, communities were deeply divided by bitter differences in religious beliefs, political positions, income inequality, legal status, and ethnic differences. Sound familiar? Jesus lived in the middle of a culture war, too. And though the political systems were different (not exactly a representative democracy), the greed, hypocrisy, and oppression of different groups used to get their way were very similar.

Jesus was born at the height of the Roman Empire's power. They'd conquered most of the known world, and Israel was no exception. Unlike previous empires that would try to destroy cultures by displacing conquered peoples' leaders, the Romans didn't force people to change their religion or customs as long as they kept their obligations to the empire. Rome would install a client king (a puppet government) and exact tribute (cash) in lots of different ways. Families were charged taxes per person—farmers on crops, fishermen on catches, and travelers were charged fees to use the roads. This was in addition to local business and religious taxes charged by priests. In Israel, political and religious factions were one and the same. Back then, it was Pharisees and Sadducees. Today, we have conservatives and liberals.

The Pharisees were the most religiously conservative leaders. They had the most influence among the common working poor, who were the majority. They believed that a king would come one day to conquer Rome with violence and free their nation. Some preyed upon a mostly illiterate population by adding extra rules and requirements that were designed to force the working poor into a posture of subjugation. The Sadducees were wealthy aristocrats who had a vested financial interest in Roman rule. They were in charge of the temple, and they didn't believe any savior king was coming. They made themselves wealthy by exacting unfair taxes and fees from the labor of their own people and by contriving money-making schemes that forced the poor to pay exorbitant prices to participate in temple sacrifice—a critical part of their religion.

There were Zealot groups who hid in the hills and violently resisted Roman occupation, and then there were the Samaritans, often oppressed and marginalized because of their racial and ethnic identities. And so, the common farmer, fisherman, or craftsman's family lived through a highly volatile political period. Overbearing religious leaders who despised and oppressed them, wealthy elites who ripped them off, racial and ethnic tension with neighbors, and sporadic violent outbreaks between an oppressive occupying army. So where was Jesus in all of this? Did he align with the religious elites? With the wealthy and powerful? Or did he start an uprising to overthrow them? None of the above.

He went from town to town, offering hope, new life, and modeling a different way to live and to change the world. Instead of pursuing power, money, or religious authority, he shared a loving and sacrificially generous way of living. He chose not to go along with the scheme's others used to impact the world. Instead, he championed a better way.

And so, each of these political groups saw him as a threat. The Pharisees recognized his movement as an affront to their authority—exposing the hypocrisy of their practices. The Sadducees saw Jesus as a threat to their power and wealth because he exposed their money-making schemes. The Zealots violently rejected one of the essential themes of Jesus' movement: love your enemy.

In the end, it took all three of these groups to have him killed. A Zealot (Judas) betrayed his location to those seeking to arrest him, the Sadducees brought him before the Romans to be executed, and when the Romans couldn't find a crime committed, the Pharisees rallied the people to force Rome's hand. Isn't it funny how political foes can come together to destroy a common enemy that threatens their designs? But in spite of their best efforts, his execution was only the beginning of a movement that continues to impact the world thousands of years later. Jesus' movement was so impactful because he actively resisted and rejected participating in culture-war politics.

Matthew 9:35-38, Luke 19:10

The future of the church is to focus on Jesus!

The story of Jesus doesn't belong to anyone,

but it has something to offer to everyone!

As we read about Jesus, we cannot help but appreciate how often he made room for the outcast, the despised, and those people that most of society deemed "weird." His inner circle of disciples, for example, were not religious scholars but blue-collar workers, fishermen, former corrupt bureaucrats, and reformed violent zealots. It was a weird crew to start a love movement, to be sure.

And there was this story about a corrupt tax man named Zacchaeus. He was reviled by his own people. A corrupt tax collector working for the foreign occupying force of the Roman Empire, he made himself wealthy by extorting and overtaxing his countrymen. Oh … and he was really short. By the time they'd crossed paths, Jesus had developed significant notoriety as a healer and a teacher. Crowds would follow him everywhere he went. When the crowd passed his way, Zacchaeus was curious to see what all the fuss was about, so he climbed a tree to see over the crowd of average-sized onlookers towering over him. And of all the people Jesus passed by, and of all the people who were following him down the path, Jesus only stopped for the odd short man that nobody liked sitting up in a tree. Weird. But powerful.

They spent time alone in his house, and their brief visit together changed Zacchaeus' life. He gave back all the money (and some) he'd extorted from his fellow oppressed citizens. People marveled at how a visit with this teacher of love forever changed that weird little person.

And we were also enamored with the story of Mary Magdalene—one of the earliest and most devoted followers of Jesus. As his movement grew, she remained a steadfast member of his inner circle, but the Bible records her history as one who was demon-possessed. Tradition ascribed even more labels to her and her past, from being a prostitute and more. My guess is she had a host of challenges, and we don't know all of them, but she certainly didn't fit the mold most people would assume characterizes a devout, loving follower of Jesus. But Jesus welcomed her with open arms, helped her overcome her issues, and gave her an important role in his movement. It was one of the many instances where people dealing with spiritual, mental, and emotional disorders—even people with a questionable past—were not just cared for, but included in Jesus' community in meaningful ways. Jesus welcomed the weird, loved the weird, and built a movement full of weirdos that ended up changing the world. The example reminds us that every person has incredible value, and their story and their identity, no matter how strange, are beautiful and important.

Jesus prioritized people. He spent much of his time with people that had terrible reputations, but he didn't seem bothered by outward appearances— when he looked at people, he looked at their hearts, and while he still saw imperfections and shortcomings, he focused on who they could be.

Take Peter for example. He was a fisherman with a hot temper who frequently made mistakes and made himself look like a fool, but Jesus trusted Peter with leadership no one else would have. He saw that Peter was capable of so much more than anyone else gave him credit. Ask yourself, how do you compare to

Jesus? How do you see yourself? Do people have the right priorities in their own life? Turns out 86% of people said they do. But when we ask that same question about others, it seems we don't give each other the benefit of the doubt. Only 28% think the people around them have their priorities well-aligned. But are our priorities actually so different? Perhaps not as much as we think.

Towards the top of many priority lists are loved ones. 90% of people said that they would sacrifice personal gain in order to benefit the people they love. 90% isn't some small faction—most of us are actually on the same page. And most of us would self-identify that we're on the same page as Jesus. 68% of people agree that Jesus could've used his ability, his power, or his influence, for personal gain, but he didn't. And another 78% of people agree that Jesus used his power and fame to set an example for those who would share his message —most of us think that Jesus gave up the opportunity for wealth, power, and influence in order to ensure that the people around him would learn to live selflessly for those around them as well. The thing that's maybe the most interesting about all of this is that Jesus acted the way most of us want to. Whether we actually act in line with our own stated priorities is a different question, but for most of us, our default desire is to live our lives in a way that puts the people we love ahead of ourselves. Jesus just happened to be very good at living his priorities out and encouraging others to do the same. Maybe we can look to him as an example of how to put our priorities into action while remembering that our priorities are not so different from other people's and even from Jesus' approach. (John 21:15-17)

For Jesus, it was issues with society at large that escalated into verbal confrontations with what we might call the religious influencers of his day — the Pharisees and the Sadducees. They made Jesus an enemy because they believed him to be a disruptive dissident who challenged their customs and character, and they were right. He strongly opposed what the Pharisees stood for and publicly scolded their hypocrisy and greed on numerous occasions. His gall shaped the Pharisees' anger, and as his following grew, so did their disdain. The elite was not the only group who had a bone to pick with Jesus. Common folk made an enemy out of him, too. Some felt that his message was too blatant, too brazen, even ludicrous. So, they took it upon themselves to make him feel unwelcome in his hometown and in cities across Israel. After all, it was an incensed crowd, not only a handful of religious elites who demanded that Pontius Pilate condemn Jesus to death. Ironically, he had famously rode into Jerusalem on a donkey a week prior, and many were ready to crown him king. However, the religious elite were quite powerful and used their influence to drown the voices of those who supported him and turned those on the fence away from him.

Jesus faced a mountain of outward enemies, but he also faced opposition from his inner circle. In arguably one of the most notorious cases of betrayal ever, Jesus had to navigate the emotional strain of being offered up to the authorities by one of his own — Judas. It was his own friend, one of his inner twelve, who led the Roman authorities to Jesus in the Garden of Gethsemane. For three years, Jesus treated Judas as a confidant, a brother. Only for Judas to later reveal himself as one of his most detrimental foes, a wolf in sheep's clothing. Jesus appeared to have a laundry list of enemies, but how did he react to those who opposed him? Well, he didn't fight fire with fire. He chose different weapons to combat his enemies — love and forgiveness. But what does that really mean? Jesus talked a lot about forgiveness, and we should focus on that all the time. (Luke 4:24-30, Matthew 26:14-16, Luke 23:3-27)

What Does This Mean?

The church exists to reach people for Christ *and* to disciple them to maturity in Christ. Both of those priorities are absolutely essential and should be practiced in harmony by each local church.

The Great Commission

The Great Commission is the direct instruction Jesus gave to his disciples to spread his teachings. In the Gospel of Mark Jesus says:

Go into all the world and preach the gospel to all creation. Whoever believes and is baptized will be saved, but whoever does not believe will be condemned. — Mark 16:15–16

Some conservative and evangelical Christians believe missionary and evangelical work still has a role to play in the spread of Christianity. They believe Christians have a duty to follow the instructions given by Jesus. They also believe they should share their religion with others so that as many people as possible can experience God's grace.

Many liberal Christians believe missionary and evangelical work is no longer as relevant as it was in the past. They may also believe that it can have a negative impact. In a multicultural society, trying to convert others might be seen as a form of *discrimination*. Liberal Christians believe that it is better to demonstrate love by accepting people's religious choices and respecting that people have different beliefs.

Today, church leaders must act as emissaries, fervently asking the Lord for discernment into how they can best practice biblically faithful ministry in their cultures and contexts.

Remember, Jesus said He would build His church. This promise should calm our fears and allow us to rest in God's mighty power to work out His purposes.

One cannot read Scripture and miss the fact it focuses on a bloody cross and an empty tomb. The gospel is about a Savior who died on a cross in our place. These are facts—not just interesting things to think or talk about—and they are usually disgusting to our neighbors. If we do not have confidence in them, then we do not have true faith and we reduce the gospel to a 12-step program for inner peace.

The gospel states, "Repentance and forgiveness of sins will be preached in his name to all nations" (Luke 24:47). Those who are confident in the gospel become living epistles, God's love letters to individuals and communities, and messages that carry the gospel's prophetic edge.

We must remove any roadblocks that keep people from getting to Jesus

If we fail to regain confidence in the gospel, subsequent generations will continue to walk away from it. Staying culturally relevant is important, and it is beneficial to minister in fresh, new ways. After all, we must remove any roadblocks that keep people from getting to Jesus. But, in the end, if strategies and systems replace the core of the gospel, its meaning and power will be lost.

We must hold firmly to our best understanding of Scripture

How do you know what to hold tightly in your right hand and what to hold loosely in your left? Granted, this is no minor task, and we need the wisdom of God to discern the difference. Essentially, you must hold firmly to your best understanding of Scripture.

We must realize that Jesus sends, and He sends us to people

Our understanding of Jesus—our Christology—will influence how we reach others. We must realize that Jesus sends, and He sends us.

We must be hopeful!

REFERENCES

The Church - First Century

1. Source: Kurtz, J. H. Church History (Vol.1-3): Complete Edition (pp. 63-64).
2. Source: John A. Apeabu (Ph.D.). Department of Christian Religious Studies, Federal College of Education, Zaria. Ii, © 2020 John A. Apeabu (Ph. D)
3. Source: Sketches of Church History, from AD 33 to the Reformation — J. C. Roberston
4. Source: What is the history and significance of the church at Jerusalem? | GotQuestions.org
5. https://en.wikipedia.org/wiki/History_of_Christianity
6. The Church – The New Churches - Source: A History of the Early Church, (05 BC-AD 451), John A. Apeabu (Ph.D.). Department of Christian Religious Studies, Federal College of Education, Zaria. Ii, © 2020 John A. Apeabu (Ph. D)
7. The Church – The New Churches - Source: A Kurtz, J. H. Church History (Vol.1-3): Complete Edition (pp. 70-71). Kindle Edition.
8. The Church – The New Churches - Source: https://www.christianity.com/wiki/bible/what-is-the-significance-of-the-church-of-ephesus-in-the-bible.html
9. The Church – The New Churches - Source: https://en.wikipedia.org/wiki/Church_of_Alexandria
10. The Church – Paul's Missionary Journeys - Source: A History of the Early Church, (05 BC-AD 451), John A. Apeabu (Ph.D.). Department of Christian Religious Studies, Federal College of Education, Zaria. Ii, © 2020 John A. Apeabu (Ph. D)
11. The Church – The Didache – 95-99 A.D.- Source: https://www.britannica.com/topic/Didache
12. The Church – The Didache – 95-99 A.D.- Source: https://www.worldhistory.org/article/904/the-didache-a-moral-and-liturgical-document-of-ins/

13. Source: Church History in Plain Language, Fifth Edition, by Bruce L. Shelley

14. Source: The Story of Christianity: Volume 1: The Early Church to the Dawn of the Reformation Kindle Edition by Justo L. González

15. Source: https://en.wikipedia.org/wiki/History_of_Christianity

16. Source: Church History 101: The Highlights of Twenty Centuries by Sinclair B. Ferguson, Joel R. Beeke, et al.

17. Source: https://www.christianity.com/church/church-history/church-history-matters-here-are-10-events-you-need-to-know.html

18. Source: https://www.christianity.com/church/church-history/church-history-matters-here-are-10-events-you-need-to-know.html

The Growing Church 100 – 300 A.D.

1. The Growing Church 100 – 300 A.D. - Source: https://www.worldhistory.org/article/904/the-didache-a-moral-and-liturgical-document-of-ins/

2. The Growing Church 100 – 300 A.D. *Jerusalem after 100 A.D.* - Source: https://atlantaserbs.com/learnmore/history/Jerusalem-church.htm

3. The Growing Church 100 – 300 A.D. *Jerusalem after 100 A.D.* - Source: A History of the Early Church, (05 BC-AD 451), John A. Apeabu (Ph.D.). Department of Christian Religious Studies, Federal College of Education, Zaria. Ii, © 2020 John A. Apeabu (Ph. D)

4. The Growing Church 100 – 300 A.D. *Jerusalem after 100 A.D.* - Source: https://en.wikipedia.org/wiki/Contra_Celsum

5. The Growing Church 100 – 300 A.D. *Jerusalem after 100 A.D.* - Source: https://www.havefunwithhistory.com/timeline-of-christian-denominations/

6. Source: A History of the Origin of the Doctrine of the Trinity in the Christian Church, by Hugh H. Stannus and R.

Spears
7. Source: Church History in Plain Language, Fifth Edition, by Bruce L. Shelley
8. Source: https://en.wikipedia.org/wiki/History_of_Christianity
9. Source: Church History 101: The Highlights of Twenty Centuries by Sinclair B. Ferguson, Joel R. Beeke, et al.

The Christian Empire 301 – 500 A.D.

1. The Christian Empire 301 – 500 A.D. - Source: https://en.wikipedia.org/wiki/Constantine_the_Great
2. The Christian Empire 301 – 500 A.D., Council of Nicaea 325 A.D. - Source: A History of the Early Church, (05 BC-AD 451), John A. Apeabu (Ph.D.). Department of Christian Religious Studies, Federal College of Education, Zaria. Ii, © 2020 John A. Apeabu (Ph. D)
3. The Growing Church 100 – 300 A.D. Council of Constantinople – 381 A.D.- Source: A History of the Early Church, (05 BC-AD 451), John A. Apeabu (Ph.D.). Department of Christian Religious Studies, Federal College of Education, Zaria. Ii, © 2020 John A. Apeabu (Ph. D)
4. The Growing Church 100 – 300 A.D. Council of Ephesus – 431 A.D. - Source: A History of the Early Church, (05 BC-AD 451), John A. Apeabu (Ph.D.). Department of Christian Religious Studies, Federal College of Education, Zaria. Ii, © 2020 John A. Apeabu (Ph. D) Source: A History of the Origin of the Doctrine of the Trinity in the Christian Church, by Hugh H. Stannus and R. Spears
5. The Growing Church 100 – 300 A.D. Council of Chalcedon – 451 A.D. - Source: A History of the Early Church, (05 BC-AD 451), John A. Apeabu (Ph.D.). Department of Christian Religious Studies, Federal College of Education, Zaria. Ii, © 2020 John A. Apeabu (Ph. D)

6. Source: https://en.wikipedia.org/wiki/History_of_Christianity

7. Source: Church History 101: The Highlights of Twenty Centuries by Sinclair B. Ferguson, Joel R. Beeke, et al.

Ancient Era to the Early Middle Ages 501-1054 A.D.

1. Second Council of Constantinople – 553 A.D. - Source: https://en.wikipedia.org/wiki/Second_Council_of_Constantinople

2. Ancient Era to the Early Middle Ages 501-1054 A.D., Second Council of Constantinople – 553 A.D. - Source: https://www.newworldencyclopedia.org/entry/Second_Council_of_Constantinople

3. Ancient Era to the Early Middle Ages 501-1054 A.D., Arab-Byzantine War, 629-644 A.D. Source: https://www.medievalists.net/2012/06/arab-byzantine-war-629-644-ad/

4. Ancient Era to the Early Middle Ages 501-1054 A.D., Continued Hostilities. Source: A History of the Early Church, (05 BC-AD 451), John A. Apeabu (Ph.D.). Department of Christian Religious Studies, Federal College of Education, Zaria. Ii, © 2020 John A. Apeabu (Ph. D)

5. Source: Church History in Plain Language, Fifth Edition, by Bruce L. Shelley

6. Source: https://en.wikipedia.org/wiki/History_of_Christianity

7. Source: Church History 101: The Highlights of Twenty Centuries by Sinclair B. Ferguson, Joel R. Beeke, et al.

The Great East-West Schism – 1054 A.D.

1. Source: https://www.learnreligions.com/the-great-schism-of-1054-4691893

2. The Great East-West Schism – 1054 A.D., Council of Constantinople – 381 A.D. - Source: A History of the Early Church, (05 BC-AD 451), John A. Apeabu (Ph.D.). Department of Christian Religious Studies, Federal College

of Education, Zaria. Ii, © 2020 John A. Apeabu (Ph. D)

3. The Great East-West Schism **Council of Clermont 1095-1571 A.D.** - Source: https://www.britannica.com/event/Council-of-Clermont

4. Source: Church History: A Complete History of the Catholic Church to the Present Day, by John Laux

5. Source: https://en.wikipedia.org/wiki/History_of_Christianity

6. Source: Church History 101: The Highlights of Twenty Centuries by Sinclair B. Ferguson, Joel R. Beeke, et al.

The Crusades 1095- 1525 A.D.

1. Source: https://crisismagazine.com/opinion/the-real-history-of-the-crusades

2. Source: Church History, by Simonetta Carr

3. Source: Church History: A Complete History of the Catholic Church to the Present Day, by John Laux

4. Source: https://en.wikipedia.org/wiki/History_of_Christianity

5. Source: Church History 101: The Highlights of Twenty Centuries by Sinclair B. Ferguson, Joel R. Beeke, et al.

The Protestant Reformation 1517 A.D. – Present Day

1. Source: https://www.khanacademy.org/humanities/renaissance-reformation/reformation-counterreformation/beginner-guide-reforrmation/a/the-protestant-reformation

2. The Protestant Reformation 1517 A.D. – Present Day - Source: A History of the Early Church, (05 BC-AD 451), John A. Apeabu (Ph.D.). Department of Christian Religious Studies, Federal College of Education, Zaria. Ii, © 2020 John A. Apeabu (Ph. D)

3. The Protestant Reformation 1517 A.D. – Present Day - Source: Christian Denominations - Source: A History of the Early Church, (05 BC-AD 451), John A. Apeabu (Ph.D.). Department of Christian Religious Studies, Federal College

of Education, Zaria. Ii, © 2020 John A. Apeabu (Ph. D)

4. Development of Eschatology – Source: https://www.logos.com/grow/what-is-eschatology/, https://www.christianity.com/, https://en.wikipedia.org/
5. Source: The Story of Christianity: Volume 1: The Early Church to the Dawn of the Reformation Kindle Edition by Justo L. González
6. Source: Church History, by Simonetta Carr
7. Source: Church History: A Complete History of the Catholic Church to the Present Day, by John Laux
8. Source: Church History 101: The Highlights of Twenty Centuries by Sinclair B. Ferguson, Joel R. Beeke, et al.

Conclusion

1. Source: https://careynieuwhof.com/10-predictions-about-the-future-church-and-shifting-attendance-patterns/
2. Conclusion - Source: https://hegetsus.com/en/articles/jesus-was-fed-up-with-politics-too?gclsrc=3p.ds&msclkid=4ad522be18f5151ac07a44e44f709b84&utm_source=bing&utm_medium=cpc&utm_campaign=LERMA%7CHAVEN%7CHGU%7CNONBRAND%7CGOOGLE%7CSEARCH%7CNAT%7CRESCON%7C&utm_term=jesus%20and%20politics%20in%20the%20bible&utm_content=Politics
3. Conclusion - Source: https://churchleaders.com/pastors/pastor-articles/151324-brady-boyd-the-future-of-the-church-4-predictions.html
4. Source: Church History, by Simonetta Carr
5. Source: Church History: A Complete History of the Catholic Church to the Present Day, by John Laux

RELIGION - HISTORY

"BUILDING THE FAITH, A HISTORY OF THE CHURCH" explores the Church from the beginning to the current age. If you have ever wondered how the Bible came into existence, how certain books were chosen, why some were not, and how doctrine was established, then perhaps this book is for you. Learn about the faith and boldness of the early church and how the gospel reached so many. This book will give you a better understanding of God's Kingdom message and how it can impact your life today!

JOSEPH CHARLES BEACH has written three books focusing on Christian values, prophecy, and history. With a strong desire to bring Holy Scripture into focus and provoke the Christian to prioritize their relationship with Jesus Christ. His prayer is that all people will come to know our truly amazing God and know Him in the most intimate way possible.